KILL BILL

AN UNOFFICIAL CASEBOOK
VOLUME TWO

KILL BILL: AN UNOFFICIAL CASEBOOK VOLUME TWO
ISBN 978-1-902588-25-4. Published 2012 by Glitter Books.
Written by D K Holm. First published 2005. Copyright © Glitter Books 2005,
2012. All world rights reserved.
CULT MOVIE FILES

Kill Bill Vol. 2 by Kim Morgan originally appeared on Reel.com.
Kill Bill Vol. 2 by David Walker first appeared in *Willamette Week* newspaper on
April 14, 2004.
Kill Bill Vol. 2 by Damon Houx originally appeared at the www.DVDJournal.com, on
August 10, 2004. Copyright © DVDJournal.com, 2004.
Mother, Killer, Warrior, Bride: Honor, Power, And Femininity in *Kill Bill* by
Jessica Harbour first appeared online at www.jessicaharbour.com. Copyright © Jessica
Harbour, 2004.
Tarantino and the Vengeful Ghosts of Cinema by Maximilian Le Cain first
appeared in *Senses of Cinema* No. 32, July-September 2004, at www.sensesof
cinema.com. Copyright © Maximilian Le Cain, June 2004.

HERE COMES THE BRIDE

Kill Bill

THE 4TH FILM BY QUENTIN TARANTINO

INTRODUCTION
WHY AN ANNOTATED "KILL BILL" BOOK?

You don't want to know what I think of Quentin Tarantino's *Kill Bill*.

If you the reader have any geek cred at all, you already know what you think. Back in the days before *Vol. 1* came out, you watched the trailer a thousand times. You maybe even downloaded the screenplay and read it carefully, although if you are a true webhead cinema geek you hate "spoilers" (see below). Later, you might have sneaked or weaseled your way into an advance screening held either for critics or the public to generate word of mouth that Miramax held about two weeks before the first part opened.

But that was way back in autumn 2003. For the next several months, you may well have contributed to one of numerous chat board forums about how much you loved *Kill Bill Vol. 1* and as a consequence read the "opinions" – i.e., the contentious, ill-thought out ramblings – of thousands more people like you. As *Kill Bill Vol. 2* rolled into sight in spring 2004, you may have (though I hope you didn't) announced to AICN.com and Chud.com or any number of other sites that *Kill Bill* will "rock" and "rule," or, more seriously, debated with like-minded posters the good and the bad, the minutia and the implications of the film. In February and then in the following August you probably bought the DVDs and have already seen them numerous times.

I know I have. I love *Kill Bill*, and this book assumes you do, too.

But whatever your level of familiarity with *Kill Bill*, you probably don't need me to confirm your assumptions or to outrage your prejudgments or to augment your own carefully vetted appraisal. You have already made up your mind.

So that's not what this book is about (necessarily). *Kill Bill: An Unofficial Casebook* is primarily an attempt, drawn from my own meager memory but mostly from scores of websites dedicated to Tarantino and *Kill Bill*, to identify all the moments of the film in which Tarantino took inspiration from other films. However, since I've put so much work into this project, I *do* reserve the right occasionally to offer up my opinions on aspects of Tarantino and his project.

Thus, there should be no mystery about the origins of or need for this book or its competitors. Quentin Tarantino's *Kill Bill* (which is what I'll call the film when referring to it as a totality, as opposed to specific partitions of *Vol. 1* or *Vol. 2*) was immediately famous, in fact even before it was made, for its carnival of referentiality. This book is for those curious about the films behind the images Tarantino chose to offer his public. In fact, as this book reveals, *Kill Bill* is probably even more referential than its first viewers suspected. Or at least people without access to the Internet. The more research I've done, the more layered *Kill Bill* appears.

Still, it is not essential that the viewer get all the references with which Tarantino has larded his film. A regular old ordinary moviegoer can get a kick out of *Kill Bill* just from its surface tale of a wronged woman seeking vengeance. Tarantino, in making an *homage* to the movies that played in the grindhouse, dollar-theater, open-24-hour, sub-run venues of his youth has made clear the fact that he wants to make a film that people can enjoy on a visceral level, that he wants to bring – dare I say it? – *jouissance* back to the moviegoing experience. The viewer's pleasure will be taken not only in the main line of the story but also the visual and narrative cleverness with which it is told.

Beyond that, however, a viewer who loves *Kill Bill* may very well want to know a lot more about it, because in the best tradition of film criticism, Tarantino's references project out from the screen only to turn around and point back to it, aiming at the immediate narrative and thematic and artistic intentions behind the references.

Most of *Kill Bill*'s references come from the quartet of genres that influenced him the most: spaghetti Westerns, martial arts films, Asian action movies, and Italian *giallos*. Tarantino made *Kill Bill* for that viewer mentioned above who just wanted a good time at the film. But that doesn't preclude the presence of interesting and complicated themes that enrich the viewer's appreciation of *Kill Bill* if alerted to their presence. In a larger sense, Tarantino is himself the perfect viewer for his own movie. He's the one who knows all the references. He is the one publicly in love with the Asian action films and spaghetti Westerns that make up the bulk of sources for its tale of revenge. But that raises another interesting question. Given that virtually every frame of the film cites some predecessor, how can we say that Tarantino is the "author"?

For the purposes of this book Tarantino will be viewed as the "author" of *Kill Bill*. He conceived the story, even if partially in collaboration, and the cast and crew were employed to realize his vision. Even if some elements of the film here or there were actually suggested by someone else, Tarantino, because the idea came from a colleague or crew member who probably shared his sensibility, will still be viewed as the suggestion's author.

Traditionally a critic might pause at this juncture to announce that this is not the time or place to enter a discussion on auteurism and its discontents. However, given Tarantino's magpie practices, this in fact is the perfect time, because how can we deem Tarantino the actual author of the film when so many of its elements are derived or inspired by a whole catalog of preceding films?

Auteurism, which began as the editorial policy of the magazine *Cahiers Du Cinema* and became the lighting rod for attack of a burgeoning film studies explosion in the early '60s, at its plainest simply offers to the critic or scholar a convenient means of cataloging the images and ideas of a film or series of films. It's understood, or should be mutually understood, that cinema, like opera and theater, is a collaborative art; but it is also suggested that a strong creative personality can impose his or her will on a series of projects that, added all together, bear the stamp of that artist despite variations in budget, personnel, and subject matter. It is also understood that some other integer besides the credited director can be the "author" of a film, such as say the writer, the producer, or even the studio, and that some "classic" films such as *Casablanca* may in fact have no central auteur at all, or, rather, so many authors that the "text" is overdetermined.

From that position we stray into two rather difficult areas. The first is that, as commercial enterprises, movies are often geared toward middlebrow expectations, received opinions of the day, or gross prejudices. The second is the notion that ultimately few movies are all that original in the first place. Parsed, the cinema of Brian De Palma, say, is really not all that different from the oeuvre of William Wellman (both return repeatedly to the plot device of a man's betrayal by his ostensive best friend). The subtle differences are fascinating to obsessives, but the works of the two are more alike than different to the average viewer, who doesn't necessarily want to follow an artist's career but rather just wants a good time at the movies.

Auteurism, as conveyed by its first American sponsor, Andrew Sarris, was, as is well known, a reaction to the ennobling sociological criticism and the films they inspired of the 1950s. To the uplifting output of Stanley Kramer (*The Defiant Ones*) and Fred Zinnemann (*High Noon*) Sarris and his acolytes (of which I am a second-generation member) offered in opposition filmmakers such as Samuel Fuller and Budd Boetticher, Fuller being an unrestrained tackler of social ills not like the more anodyne Kramer, while Boetticher used the Western genre to ponder the subtle hierarchies of men in conflict.

Auteur filmmakers weren't good for you. They raised depressing issues and didn't have a hell of a lot of answers. They tended to dwell in the slime pit of twisted urges and bad luck, like a sap in an Edgar G. Ulmer film. Auteur critics favored genres over homogenized mainstream studio product, and vivacity over calm reasoning. Reviewers at the time such as Pauline Kael and Dwight Macdonald hated it, not because they weren't auteurists in their own manner, but because the young, brash auteur writers favored, or appeared to favor, action films over, say, musicals and screwball comedies or inspiring Soviet realist films. (Paradoxically, Tarantino's favorite movie reviewer has always been Kael rather than Sarris, and he supposedly can quote reams of her *New Yorker* reviews, a state of affairs I find it difficult to reconcile myself to.) And even when various Gallic imports took over academia in the 1970s, the Pantheon (Chaplin, Flaherty, Ford, Griffith, Hawks, Hitchcock, Keaton, Lang, Lubitsch, Murnau, Ophuls, Renoir, von Sternberg, Welles) and near-Pantheon directors (Aldrich, Fuller, Karlson, Mann and many, many others) that Sarris listed, and some of the key films they made (*Young Mr. Lincoln*, *Bringing Up Baby*, *Touch Of Evil*), continued to be the subject matter of film scholars who denied the efficacy of the auteur approach, who ceased to believe in authors.

It was only a matter of time before filmmakers who shared these directorial enthusiasms would pay their respects in their own films. (Not that friendly salutes between filmmakers were uncommon before the 1960s, for which see the visual complements between Ford's *The Searchers* and Hawks's *The Big Sky*.) First the French New Wave directors, especially Tarantino favorite Jean-Luc Godard, peppered their films with citations to their influences and inspirations. Then a host of American filmmakers who were truly

8

independent (back when that word meant something) such as Brian De Palma and Martin Scorsese paid fealty to the filmmakers who helped them solve technical problems (Hitchcock) or who first created an affecting mood that they were trying to recreate (Fellini).

Tarantino, as a Godardo-Hawksian, takes as his birthright the option to quote from his elders, either as an act of fealty or as an attempt to improve, provide a variation on, or examine more closely certain cinematic ideas. Tarantino came of age just as sampling became prevalent in rap and hip-hop music and from the artistic side of his brain (as opposed to the commercial side that might seek to be protective of copyrights and ownership), Tarantino appears to take the view that anything in the culture is up for grabs, i.e., a very Elizabethan attitude to intellectual property rights.

Which brings us, in a way, to the subject of spoilers. As many visitors to the World Wide Web will know, spoilers are a particular fixation of writers and readers. If a writer dare tread anywhere near the brink of actually revealing meaningful things about the plot of a movie, she or he *must*, by common consent, flash a spoiler alert, like the Fear Flasher and Horror Horn in *Chamber Of Horrors*, a SIDS monitor designed to keep the blank slate mind of the infantalized potential viewers shielded in the swaddling clothes of ignorance. Meanwhile, these same spoiler-phobic readers devour trailers, which, the last time I viewed one, revealed pretty much everything that was going to appear in the film. And indeed, the raison d'etre of most websites is to "spoil" things – to make information easily accessible, to describe things fast and early. The whole function of Harry Knowles's Ain't It Cool News in its early days was to spring early information about movies and screenings on readers. Now its TalkBack writers feud with each other on this or that "spoiled" plot point. To dread spoilers yet tread obsessively through cyberspace is to live a contradiction.

For the record, then, everything in this book is a spoiler. It is written under the assumption that you have seen *Kill Bill* several times and want to know more about the film. It is not for neophytes. Nor is this book, like any Cliffs Notes, a substitution for watching the film.

Tarantino raids the culture for inspiration. Therefore, to fully appreciate *Kill Bill* as a cultural artifact, as opposed to an entertainment, the serious film student needs to see just as many films as Tarantino himself – or have an available trot, such as this one. That, or access to a very well-stocked video store.

Yet ultimately, *Kill Bill* must work as an entertainment if it is to have an afterlife. The inspiration for the interested viewer to dig deeper into the film's sources is the pleasure that the film itself, shorn of its influences, provides. If I may paraphrase my betters, a man goes to the theater to enjoy a film, to escape everyday worries as well as to be engaged in a good solid intellectual puzzle (themes, image clusters, repetition, variation). The squirrel-scholar annotator must acknowledge that he is that man.

A Few Notes For The Reader

The central portion of this book – the second of two volumes – is a series of annotations keyed to the time codes of *Kill Bill Vol. 2* as found on the North American Region 1 DVD. The time codes for specific moments are not necessarily always exact, but they will get you to the right frames under discussion or annotation.

For this book I have read numerous other volumes, all listed in the bibliography, seen scores of movies, and visited dozens of websites. Without all these resources and the hundreds of enthusiastic Tarantino posters, this endeavor would have been unlikely. In many cases, it is impossible to track down who said what first.

We have reached a stage where it is truly appropriate to say that everybody's a critic. I can't tell you the number of times that I thought I had a key critical insight or made an interesting connection only to browse through a website's chat forum and find that someone else had made the same connection months earlier. The public may be at a level of "critical mass" that meets or exceeds that of the professional movie reviewer. No wonder so many cinematic brainiacs flee to the groves of academe, where they can burrow into arcana with a vocabulary no one can else can follow. In fact, the reader might be better off assuming that nothing in this book is original, that the author is a film-critical version of Tarantino himself, inspired and lifting from everything.

I don't claim to have tracked down every reference in *Kill Bill*. I don't have all the answers, and I am sure I've got some things dead wrong (I dread yet would find most helpful a *Video Watchdog* review). But the movie is fun to think about, and I am open to suggestions, corrections, speculations, which can be directed to <dkholm@mac.com>.

The History Of Kill Bill

Numerous articles about the movie have traced its genesis. *Kill Bill* had its roots in discussions that Tarantino had with Uma Thurman on the set of *Pulp Fiction*. In that film, Thurman played a gangster's moll who once starred in a TV pilot. The mythical show was called *Fox Force Five*. He began to collaborate with Thurman on the concept of The Bride, a member of a team like Fox Force Five, who is attacked by her colleagues and left for dead, only to come after them for revenge. Tarantino's intentions were to make it the ultimate Saturday matinee movie, the perfect grindhouse revenge film, a celebration of the junk he loved as a kid, and still loved. He says that he began writing *Kill Bill* while in New York City, and once left his notebook with the sole draft of the script in the back of a cab and had to run down the cab.

Apparently Tarantino tinkered with the script and eventually put it away. But a chance encounter with Thurman backstage at an awards ceremony reignited his interest in the project. He vowed he would finish the script and is supposed to have delivered it to her on her birthday (August 22), probably in the year 2000. Miramax got behind the production, and after extensive location scouting in the United States, Mexico, and Asia, shooting was set to begin in spring 2001. Thurman's unexpected pregnancy delayed production however, for several months. She didn't show up on the set until March 2002. Filming began in Bejing Film Studio in June 2002 and lasted in that studio for four months. Tarantino wanted to use the Shaw Brothers studio, now mostly used for television, but it wasn't big enough (though Tarantino got to visit Run Run Shaw's private screening room while there). The bulk of the House of Blue Leaves section was shot during an unusually long time, followed by the scenes with martial arts master Pai Mei in his mountain temple, followed by the scenes in Hattori Hanzo's sushi shop. The final footage shot in China was between The Bride and Sofie Fatale around the trunk of her car. In early September the crew transplanted itself to Tokyo for a few nights of street shooting, and then moved to Pasadena, California, for the scenes between The Bride and Vernita Green. The production then moved to other locations in California, Texas, and finally Mexico, in all comprising 155 days of shooting (or about as many shooting days as *Terminator 2*).

Originally planned as a single film derived from a 197-page

screenplay, Miramax decided in summer 2003 (after some subtle prompting from Tarantino) to issue the film in two parts, the first in October, the second in February 2004 (later pushed back to May).

Making any kind of movie requires great dedication, but the lengthy production schedule of *Kill Bill* suggests monumental commitment on the order of a David Lean. What was it about this project that so goaded Tarantino to action after several years of silence?

There are several possibilities. As is well known, Tarantino is a great borrower, and there were authorship disputes over *Pulp Fiction* recounted in the three bios about Tarantino that came out in the mid-'90s. After the "failure" of *Jackie Brown* (more apparent than real), Tarantino went into seclusion in this new well-acquitted estate. As mentioned, among the tasks he appears to have set for himself was an immersion in American film directors, which led to his revival of interest in William Witney.

I think that among the other things he was doing while in seclusion was hunkering down and truly writing a screenplay, on his own. He did at least two, and this activity was a middle finger in the face of the detractors who cast suspicions on whether he really writes his scripts, such as Jane Hamsher in her book *Killer Instinct*, about the making of *Natural Born Killers*. In that memoir Hamsher reprints a note Tarantino sent her that she offers up as evidence of Tarantino's supposed illiteracy and therefore, by inference, his inability to write the scripts credited to him. I would speculate that Tarantino, with his long *Inglorious Basterds* script and with *Kill Bill* (but not the Elmore Leonard Western adaptation he was also supposedly doing) was making a definitive statement that he is a *writer*-director, not just a director.

But I also wonder if Tarantino has really, aside from discoveries such as Witney, given up on American movies. *Kill Bill* is derived mostly from Italian and Asian movies, and perhaps Hollywood as an entertainment industry has abandoned him as much as it has abandoned viewers who are a lot like him. He noted in one interview at the time that he had immersed himself in Japanese films by Takashi Miike and others. There he finds the truth and cinematic style missing in Hollywood "product." America is too big, its profit margins too narrow, its need to cater to the mediocre middlebrow mindset and avoid extremes and variety too great. It seems only fitting to note that the remake of the *Texas Chainsaw*

Massacre made in its first weekend almost as much money as *Kill Bill* did in three.

Still, *Kill Bill* is having a more long lasting effect on the culture. Cinema fanatics are still crazy about it. Hence this book.

Four weeks into its release, I was amazed at how often *Kill Bill* still came up in conversation. Discussions about other films released around the time (such *School Of Rock*, *Elephant*, *Master and Commander: The Far Side Of The World*, *Timeline*, *Shattered Glass*) always seemed to lead back to *KB*. It became a benchmark by which to judge other new movies.

One chilly night in late November of 2003 I was meeting with my weekly Thursday night group of film geeks and movie writers, huddled in the unheated smokey back room of a neighborhood bar. The subject of *Kill Bill* came up again, as it usually did, along with *Lord Of The Rings: The Return Of The King*, other new films and whatever big DVD was coming out that week or the next that everyone wanted. Someone asked, "How many times have you seen it?" One fellow said twice. I said three times. Another colleague said five times. And so on. The movie hadn't been out all that long, but we had already seen it multiple times

It's that kind of movie. You want to see it again and again. You return to it like comfort food during a cinematic wasteland. Then and there we all made plans to see it together again once *Kill Bill* hit one of those beer and pizza theaters so prominent in my home town. I can add now that in the course of compiling this book I've seen *Kill Bill* an additional innumerable times, yet not once tired of it. In fact, there is still the danger, when I pop in the DVD to check a fact, that I will be waylaid by a scene and watch it or the whole damn film through to the end, and beyond. If this book is late to the stores, that's the reason.

KILL BILL

A ROARING RAMPAGE OF REVENGE
THE 4TH FILM BY QUENTIN TARANTINO

ONE
"KILL BILL" VOL. 2 : ANNOTATIONS

Time Code: 0:00:01
Information: Sound cue, "A Silhouette of Doom."

By Ennio Morricone, from *Un Dollaro A Testa*, or *For A Few Dollars More* (1965), Leone's second "Dollars" movie with Clint Eastwood and Lee Van Cleef.

The music begins over the Miramax logo and progresses on from there.

Time Code: 0:00:015
Information: Dialogue, "Do you find me sadistic?"

Along with The Bride's panting, this dialogue is a reiteration of the first film.

This introductory material is, of course, not likely to survive a fusing of the two films back together. It concludes at 00:00:46 with the shot to the head, The Bride attempting to play her one trump card by revealing that the baby she is carrying is Bill's.

Time Code: 0:00:55
Information: Dialogue, "Looked dead, didn't I?"

The film officially opens with black-and-white footage of The Bride, wearing a black leather jacket, driving what must be a Karmann Ghia (given what she says here and what we see at the end of the film). This material is supposedly meant to appear at the start of the full version of the film.

Tarantino likes rear projection car scenes. He has used it to most dramatic effect in *Pulp Fiction*, when a dreamy Vincent is driving under the influence, and when Esmeralda is driving Butch in the cab (the background representing no attempt to be realistic, but being derived from old movies).

This material appeared in the teasers and trailers for *Kill Bill*

Vol. 2.

Time Code: 0:01:09
Information: Dialogue, "I went on what the movie advertisements refer to as a roaring rampage of revenge."

Both *Bury Me An Angel* (1971) and *Foxforce* (mentioned above) use this phrase in their advertising. *Bury Me An Angel* is a female revenge film directed by Barbara Peeters and starring Dixie Peabody as a biker chick out to punish her brother's killer. Its poster's tagline reads, "She's a Howling Hellcat Humping a Hot Steel Hog on a Roaring Rampage of Revenge!"

Time Code: 0:01:15
Information: Dialogue, "I roared."

The Bride is a lioness. The end of the movie shows The Bride "back with her cub."

Time Code: 0:01:26
Information: Dialogue, "But I have only one more."

This line situates The Bride on the "road to Salina." That is, The Bride, chronologically speaking, has just left Esteban Vihaio and is heading toward Bill's villa.

Time Code: 0:01:44
Information: Music cue,

Morricone's "A Silhouette Of Doom" reaches its searing crescendo as the title "Vol. 2" rolls up from the bottom of the screen.

Time Code: 0:02:03
Information: Title card, "Chapter Six Massacre at Two Pines."

Originally, this section was going to comprise a scene in which Bill takes out a gambling house matron. Over the course of both preproduction and the production itself Tarantino constantly rewrote and added to the script, adding roles for people he knew or just met and liked. Jeannie Epper is an example of that. See below.

The chapel is found on Aqua Caliente Street, which is also the name of a town in *For A Few Dollars More*.

Furthermore, Two Pines is also the name of the mall in *Back To The Future*. Tarantino was once jointly interviewed with that film's director, Robert Zemeckis.

Time Code: 0:02:48
Information: Image, the wedding party.

Our first good view of the interior of the chapel and the participants, the corpses "later" to be scattered about the premises. The attendees in this shot are The Bride, Tommy Plympton (in real special-effects technician Chris Nelson, and who bears a resemblance to Chevy Chase), Joleen (Stephanie L. Moore), Janeen (Caitlin Keats), and Erica (Shana Stein), plus the Reverend Harmony (Bo Svenson), his wife (stuntwoman Jeannie Epper), and Rufus, the piano player (Samuel L. Jackson). There is also an unidentified male visible in some shots, standing behind the girls.

As is typical with Tarantino, the Reverend's chat to the group preceded the visuals inside the chapel.

Time Code: 0:02:54
Information: Image, the Reverend Harmony and his wife.

Our first visual of the preacher and his wife. Bo Svenson is a Swedish-Russian immigrant who came to the United States in his teenage years. He was an athlete at UCLA and made his debut in the TV series *Here Come The Brides* in 1968. His cult credentials are due to taking over the Joe Don Baker role for *Walking Tall Part II*, but he has also appeared in *Heartbreak Ridge* and *North Dallas Forty*. As far as Tarantino connections go, he appeared in the Italian WWII film *Inglorious Bastards* (1978), one of Tarantino's favorites.

Jeannie Epper is a longtime stuntwoman who has appeared in several Jack Hill films, including *Coffy* and *Switchblade Sisters*, where she has a small part as a prison matron. She can be seen most recently in the documentary about female stunt Zoë Bell, *Double Dare*.

Time Code: 0:03:10
Information: Image, Rufus, from the rear.

He offers to play "Love Me Tender," the Elvis hit from 1956. Elvis Presley is a special favorite of Tarantino's and makes an appearance in his script for *True Romance*.

Time Code: 0:03:24
Information: Dialogue, "Rufus, he's the Man."

Later, Bill says that *he* is the Man.

Time Code: 0:03:36
Information: Dialogue, "I was a Drell. I was a Drifter. I was a Coaster. I was part of the Gang. I was a Barkay."

Rufus runs down his resume. He's played with Rufus Thomas (1917–2001), the Mississippi-born "world's oldest teenager" and a blues, soul, and funk musician. In addition he's played with Archie

Bell and the Drells, The Drifters ("Up On The Roof"), The Coasters ("Yakety Yak"), Kool and the Gang, and The Barkays ("Soul Finger"). If you are wondering why a musician with such an illustrious past as Rufus would be living in El Paso and playing a church piano, it may be that Rufus never actually toured with these groups but played backup with them for a night when they performed in the town, a not-uncommon practice.

> **Time Code**: 0:04:00
> **Information:** Dialogue, "Thank you, Mother."

The Reverend Harmony is a square, calling his wife "Mother" as older generations did (Svenson does the take brilliantly, however). His doing so, however, fits in with the motherhood theme of the film and The Bride's quest.

> **Time Code**: 0:05:01
> **Information:** Image, The Bride leaning back to talk to her friends.

Mrs. Harmony is bugging The Bride, and this scene hints at the anger that bristles under the weight of conventionality and mediocrity that may have made her subject to Bill's seductions.

The moment also allows the audience's first view of Caitlin Keats. The young actress (31) has a ravishing smile and, like Julie Dreyfus in the first film, has inspired numerous fanboy crushes. Her other films include *Murder In Small Town X* and *The Good Humor Man*. She has also appeared in an Olay commercial.

> **Time Code**: 0:05:20
> **Information:** Image and sound cue, The Bride walking out, then hearing the flute.

The Bride goes from happiness to alarm in a matter of a few moments.

> **Time Code**: 0:05:26
> **Information:** Music cue, Ennio Morricone's "Il Tramonte (Sundown)."

From *Il Buono, Il Brutto, Il Cattivo*, or *The Good The Bad*

And The Ugly (1966). This beautiful theme plays when Sentenza, the Lee Van Cleef character, is introduced.

Time Code: 0:05:28
Information: Image, the open door of the chapel, with the desert outside.

A quite obvious reference to John Ford's *The Searchers* (1956), in which John Wayne and Jeffrey Hunter are in a five-year hunt for a family member kidnapped by Sioux — Wayne to kill her, Hunter to save her from him. It's one of Ford's darker, most tense films, with an uneasy blend of humor and horror, essentially an incoherent text, but all the more fascinating to watch for that.

In 1979, Stuart Byron wrote in *New York* magazine about the startling influence of *The Searchers*, then a Ford film only beginning to appear on ten-best lists among "New Hollywood" directors. He charted how visual references, plot points, and general structures from *The Searchers* found their way into films by Scorsese (*Who's That Knocking At My Door?*, *Mean Streets*, *Taxi Driver*), Spielberg (*Close Encounters Of The Third Kind*), Schrader (*Hardcore*), Milius (*Big Wednesday*, *The Wind And The Lion*), Cimino (*The Deer Hunter*), and Lucas (*Star Wars*). Tarantino is now in this tradition. It's a fascinating article and well worth digging up.

At 00:05:50, the camera tracks up, and The Bride enters screen right, framed by the door, a further iteration of the *Searchers* connection.

Time Code: 0:06:06
Information: Image, the first full view of Bill.
There is some cross-cutting between the two, then Bill looks up and says, "Hello, kiddo."
We all now know that this is an in-joke, of course.
The large wooden flute Bill is playing resembles the instrument David Carradine plays as Kwai Chang Caine in the international hit TV series *Kung Fu* and later in *Circle Of Iron* (1978), a martial arts movie in which Carradine plays four parts.

Time Code: 0:06:45
Information: Dialogue, "I'm the Man."

For the role of Bill, the Machiavellian puppeteer and master of the DiVAS, Tarantino settled on David Carradine, the now-grizzled former hippie icon who was once the role model for 1970s preteen boys thanks to the series *Kung Fu*.

David Carradine in 2002 was a 65-year-old actor and author. Like Peter Fonda and Michael Sarrazin, he was one of those big, lanky, lumpy, good-looking guys who in another, prehippie generation would have played doctors on NBC medical shows. The offspring of an actor, John Carradine, he has three acting half-brothers, Robert and Keith, and also Michael Bowen, who also appears in the film (and may have been a connection between Tarantino and Carradine).

Carradine *pere* was a notable character actor, frequently seen in John Ford films (*The Grapes Of Wrath*), but also a horror film mainstay (he appeared as Dracula in *House Of Frankenstein*). The elder Carradine died in 1988, leaving behind, among other things, three ex-wives and three sons following his example.

Carradine was born in 1936 and was educated at San Francisco State before entering the movie business in 1964 with the film *Taggart*. Two years later, he garnered the lead in a short-lived television series, *Shane*. Middling exploitation films followed, but he achieved international popularity thanks to the role of Kwai Chang Caine in *Kung Fu*, which blended faux Eastern philosophy with fight scenes, the essentially peaceful Caine always goaded into violence against his beliefs, a la Billy Jack. The series lasted three seasons, and its cultural importance looms larger than its financial success. The prolific performer then appeared in numerous films, from the Roger Corman-produced *Death Race 2000* and *Deathsport* (notoriously, the film on whose set cocaine was reintroduced to the movie industry), to *Bound For Glory*, a biopic about Woody Guthrie, for which Carradine received an Oscar nomination.

Carradine's appeal for Tarantino resided not only in his having appeared in *Kung Fu*, but also because he appeared in other cult martial arts films, such as *Circle Of Iron* and Scorsese's *Boxcar Bertha*. Carradine came with a built in-hippie-bred sympathy with Asian philosophy, and his name is attached to several books on martial arts, *Spirit Of Shaolin: A Kung Fu Philosophy* (from Charles Tuttle publishers), and *David Carradine's Tai Chi Workout* (Henry Holt).

Tarantino has praised Carradine's versatile, chameleon face

in interviews, and also indicated that reading Carradine's autobiography, *Endless Highways*, helped inspire him to hire the actor after Beatty fell out.

Time Code: 0:07:27
Information: Dialogue, "I've never been nice my whole life."

Bill — a father figure of a man who is himself fatherless and always looking for father figures — reassures The Bride that he'll be "sweet" (in John Carradine's marvelously lispy and growly voice). When The Bride's groom, Tommy Oliphant, invites Bill to give away The Bride, you get a hint of anticipatory menace from Carradine as he says, "That's asking a lot." The pure understated force of the way he says it reminds me of Steve Buscemi as Tony Blundetto in *The Sopranos* telling Tony Soprano in an early episode from its fifth season, "You're crowding me."

Time Code: 0:07:37
Information: Image, The Bride's sandaled feet, walking toward Bill.

This is matched by Bill's cowboy boots walking toward The Bride. A common enough trope and not necessarily related to Tarantino's foot fetish.

Time Code: 0:07:50
Information: Dialogue, "A bun in the oven."

Another example of Tarantino's colloquial phraseology.

Time Code: 0:07:57
Information: Dialogue, "Jeeze, Louise."

As is this.

Time Code: 0:08:33
Information: Dialogue, "What does your young man do for a living?"

The first introduction in *Vol. 2* of the theme of work. Tommy, it turns out, owns a record store in El Paso. When Bill asks her what The Bride is doing for a "J.O.B." these days," we learn that The Bride works in the record store, opening up whole potentialities of backstory. Bill says, "A-so," and that it "all suddenly seems so clear." Is that the feeling that Tarantino wants to create in the viewer?

"J.O.B." also spells out Job, which may well be one of Tarantino's several subtle references to the Bible. At the very least, The Bride's sufferings certainly compete with Job's.

Time Code: 0:09:13
Information: Dialogue, "I get to listen to music all day."

The Bride, explaining why she likes her job. These views reflect Clarence Worley's in *True Romance* about working in a comic-book store, and in turn probably reflect Tarantino's about working in a video store.

Time Code: 0:09:28
Information: Dialogue," As opposed to jetting around the world, killing human beings and being paid vast sums of money?"

Bill leans in when he says this, the first hint of the ire that he must feel, the hint of why he is mad at The Bride, why he "overreacts," as he says later.

Time Code: 0:09:47
Information: Dialogue, "All cockblockery aside."

J. E. Lighter's *Random House Historical Dictionary of American Slang* (1994) defines "cockblock" as "to thwart the sexual advances of (a third person)."

Time Code: 0:09:55
Information: Dialogue, "I happen to be more or less particular whom my gal marries."

From Howard Hawks's *His Girl Friday* (1940), spoken by Cary Grant's character Walter Burns about Rosalind Russell's Hildy Johnson, his ex-wife.

Time Code: 0:010:06
Information: Dialogue, "You'll find it a bit lonely on my side." "Your side always was a bit lonely."

A hint at the metaphysical connection between The Bride and Bill, two lonely solo warriors who let down their guard with each other, if only briefly — a familiar romantic entanglement in martial arts films.

Time Code: 0:10:20
Information: Dialogue, "I had the loveliest dream about you."

He doesn't get a chance to tell it. If he had, might he have spared The Bride? Tommy interrupts, and, in screwball comedy style, The Bride quickly tells Bill to call her Arlene.

Time Code: 0:10:33
Information: Dialogue," Tommy, I'd like you to meet my father."

Carradine's take on this is hilarious.

Time Code: 0:10:44
Information: Dialogue, "The name's Bill."

Bill Machiavelli?

Time Code: 0:10:57
Information: Dialogue, "In the surprise department the apple doesn't fall far from the tree."

More common man phraseology.

Time Code: 0:11:04
Information: Dialogue, "Did you come straight from Australia?" and "Daddy, I told him you were in Perth mining for silver."

This seemingly innocuous dialogue (is Bill a "silver surfer"?) foreshadows the book by Jasmine Yuen that Esteban Vihaio is reading at the end of the film.

Time Code: 0:11:29
Information: Dialogue, "Why pay so much money for a dress that you're only gonna wear once?"

Tommy's justification for a wedding dress rehearsal raises the money-work-thrift issue again, but The Bride's dedication to her new love can be measured by her imperviousness to these concerns.

Time Code: 0:11:40
Information: Dialogue, "Isn't it supposed to be bad luck for the groom to see the bride in her wedding dress before the ceremony?"

Yes, it is and it will be. The superstition dates back to the early 1900s when the concept of the wedding dress was introduced.

Fate, happenstance, and luck are perennial concerns here and elsewhere in Tarantino's work, fuel for narrative twists, such as Butch happening to see Wallace outside his apartment. Martial arts films are especially dependent on luck, that tool lying there easily converted to a weapon, or this chance encounter unveiling unexpected events. In *Kill Bill* The Bride's happening to get pregnant is the spur to the rest of the plot.

Time Code: 0:11:48
Information: Dialogue, "Well, I guess I just believe in living dangerously."

Tommy leans in like William Hurt. He also talks with his finger pointing, like a gun. Aggression in *Kill Bill* world is pandemic.

Time Code: 0:12:09
Information: Dialogue, "That's not exactly Daddy's cup of tea."

Another average Joe cliché.

Time Code: 0:12:17
Information: Dialogue, "That's asking a lot."

This phrase has defeated your author. I had a suspicion that the line came from somewhere, perhaps a Hawks film, and that suspicion was confirmed when I saw a citation of it in a Tarantino forum. Unfortunately, I didn't immediately write it down, and amid the chaos of research and writing, I couldn't dig it up again. I am praying that some kindly reader will e-mail me the solution to this puzzle.

Time Code: 0:12:29
Information: Dialogue, "Only on the condition that I pay for everything."

Money again. Bill's largesse, at this moment, probably renders him very attractive to Tommy.

Time Code: 0:12:51
Information: Music cue, Rufus playing the piano.

As The Bride runs up to Bill to thank him … for what? Not killing Tommy?

By the way, the DVD subtitles announce guitar rather than piano playing.

Time Code: 0:12:58
Information: Dialogue, "You don't owe me a damn thing."

Another defeat. I am sure this is from somewhere. On the other hand, it may be a common enough phrase in many post-'60s Westerns.

Time Code: 0:13:10
Information: Image, The Bride kisses Bill.

One of the few tender moments in the film. There are very few kisses in the Tarantino oeuvre. Like Welles and Kubrick, he tends to shy away from kissing, much less explicit sex.

Time Code: 0:13:23
Information: Music cue, "Dies Irae"

Written by Nora Orlandi and performed by Paolo Ormi.

Time Code: 0:13:46
Information: Image, The Bride kisses Bill again and says thank you.

Which brings up the interesting question, when did Bill decide to kill The Bride? Was it before he arrived at the chapel? Was it during his conversation with The Bride? Or when he met Tommy? Or when he decided to sit on the bride's side of the church? Or when she kissed him a second time?

Was his sitting on the bride's side a "signal" to those waiting outside to come in and finish what he started?

And how joyous were the others to participate? Vernita, angry because The Bride had the codename Black Mamba, *her* rightful name (a surface issue masking a more deep-seated resentment?). O-Ren doing to another what was once done to her. Budd, secretly in love with his brother, perhaps, eager to eliminate The Bride because she "broke my brother's heart." And Elle, perhaps during the past three or four months managing to rise in ascendancy, working Iago-like on Bill and quickening his heart against The Bride. He might have forgiven her. He even had "the nicest dream" about her on the eve of the very day he plans to kill her. Elle, as is proven later, is a blithe liar.

Time Code: 0:13:50
Information: Image, a crane shot backwards and out of the chapel.

At 00:14:08, the gang appears. Budd slides into the frame, from left. They are, in order, Vernita, Budd, O-Ren, and Elle. At 00:14:22 they walk into the chapel, at which point Reverend Harmony says, "What the hell?"

This is the fourth oath in the church. Earl, his son, and Tommy, who says "Goddamn," all curse.

Through the windows of the chapel you get a glimpse of what's happening. The four friends try to run to their left.

Is Sofie Fatale there?

This scene finds part of its inspiration from the opening of *The Good The Bad And The Ugly*. In that scene, the saddle tramp character hunting Stucco Ramirez (Eli Wallach) hooks up with two other gunmen and they storm the restaurant where Tucco is eating. In both films, people are laying in wait outside a place, with the subsequent action occurring inside and off-screen.

Time Code: 0:15:14
Information: Dialogue, "There wasn't really 88 of 'em."

How many were there? Our no-doubt inaccurate count is found above.

Time Code: 0:15:14
Information: Image, Bill, with his car in the right background.

Bill appears in a stylish black suit, and behind him is an equally stylish black De Tomaso Mangusta, a rarity among muscle cars (only 400 were manufactured back in 1969). Meanwhile, Budd wears a straw Stetson, bears tattoos, has a razor blade dangling on a chain around his neck, and is spitting his chaw into a can while sitting in the doorway of his rundown trailer. A certain class difference is suggested, even though theoretically they are both the sons of whores and raised by Esteban.

Time Code: 0:15:31
Information: Dialogue, "Didn't he swear a blood oath to never make another sword?"

More backstory. The reason that Hattori Hanzo stopped making swords is because of Bill and the use he put them to.

Madsen is so closely identified with Tarantino that it comes as a surprise that *Kill Bill* represents only the second time he has worked with the director. He almost appeared in *Pulp Fiction* (there was a conflict with *Wyatt Earp*), and out of loyalty to Tarantino he declined to appear in *Natural Born Killers.* Madsen is a fascinating contemporary screen presence because he is a throwback to an older style of movie, evoking a resemblance to Robert Mitchum, whom he reveres and with whom he shares a penchant for poetry (Madsen has

published four collections). Born in Chicago in 1958, Madsen is the son of a firefighter. He got his start in Chicago's Steppenwolf Theater, and later followed his sister, Virginia Madsen, out to Hollywood. After some 13 films, including *The Natural* (1984), Madsen broke into public consciousness with his villainous turn in *Kill Me Again* (1989) and as Susan Sarandon's near-perfect boyfriend in *Thelma And Louise* (1991). With his turn as the copy-heating Mr. Blonde-Vic Vega in *Reservoir Dogs* he became a cult favorite. He went on to appear in *Free Willy* (1993), the remake of *The Getaway* (1994), *Species* (1995), and *The Last Days Of Frankie The Fly* (1997) with Dennis Hopper and Daryl Hannah. Arguably his best performance is in *Donnie Brasco* (1997), with Al Pacino and Johnny Depp. He's a busy actor, making about four movies a year. He played Blood in *Beyond The Law* (1992) and lived in a trailer.

Madsen has a commanding physical presence that you can only define as cool. His improvised soda cup prop in *Reservoir Dogs* suggested the Hemingway-esque grace under pressure that is the hallmark of the cinematic cool character, and the equally improvised whisper into the severed cop's ear bespeaks a sharp mind and cruel wit. He is a tall man but acts "small," with the tic of crinkling his forehead and looking up from a duck as if he were constantly crouching under obstructions or those around him. Tarantino writes good roles for Madsen, and he acts them in career-defining ways.

Budd is named after Budd Boetticher, the film director who died in 2001 at the age of 85. He is most famous for the run of Westerns he made with Randolph Scott in the '50s, including *The Tall T* (1957), *The Name's Buchanan* (1958), *Ride Lonesome* (1959), and *Comanche Station* (1960). Boetticher was a major influence on Leone, and his films are characterized by the tense and intricate confrontations between good men and bad as they jostle each other for authority during enforced cohabitation. Andrew Sarris wrote sympathetically of Boetticher in his book, *The American Cinema*, "One wonders where directors like Boetticher find the energy and the inspiration to do such fine work, when native critics are so fantastically indifferent."

Bill and Budd taken together make Billy Budd, the title character in a story by Herman Melville. According to one biographer, Tarantino's mother read Melville to him as a child.

Time Code: 0:15:42
Information: Dialogue, "Them Japs sure know how to hold a grudge, don't they."

In a few seconds, he says he doesn't "dodge guilt, and I don't Jew out of paying my comeuppance" (elided, by the way, in the making-ofs on the DVD). In contrast to Bill's high-class sophistication, Budd is an angry, racist slob, yet Tarantino manages to elicit sympathy from us for him.

Time Code: 0:15:50
Information: Dialogue, "Or maybe, you just tend to bring that out in people."

This hints at the tragedy that is Bill.

Time Code: 0:16:07
Information: Dialogue, "I pawned that [Hanzo sword] years ago."

This is a lie, of course, designed to needle Bill. We see the sword later.

Time Code: 0:16:24
Information: Dialogue," Not in El Paso it ain't."

This is where Budd supposedly pawned his sword. Why El Paso, and why did he hock it "years ago"? Was that four years ago? Was Budd disturbed by the events at the Two Pines Chapel? Tarantino, like Polanski, likes to leave most of his backstory unexplained.

Time Code: 0:16:50
Information: Dialogue, "And the last time we spoke wasn't the most pleasant."

More mysterious backstory.

Time Code: 0:16:59
Information: Dialogue, the name of The Bride is bleeped

out again.

This is the fourth bleeping of The Bride's name.

Time Code: 0:17:13 – 00:18:16
Information: Music cue, a reprise of "Dies Irae."

Written by Nora Orlandi and performed by Paolo Ormi – as Budd talks to Bill.

Time Code: 0:17:31
Information: Dialogue, "Can't we just forget the past?"

Nice try. Revenge films are contingent upon the inability to forget the past or forgive a slight.

Time Code: 0:18:08
Information: Image, My Oh My club,

The "titty bar" where Budd works as a bouncer. Note that there is a white Honda in the lot, another signature Tarantino object that appears in *Pulp Fiction* and *Jackie Brown*, 00:18:26.

Time Code: 0:18:12
Information: Title card, "Chapter Seven, The Lonely Grave of Paula Shultz."

I haven't seen *The Wicked Dreams of Paula Schultz*, a romantic sex comedy from 1968 starring Elke Sommer as Paula, an Olympic champ who jumps the Berlin wall, and Bob Crane as, significantly or not, Bill, the guy who helps her out (the film reunites the *Hogan's Heroes* lead with his co-star Werner Klemperer). It's directed by George Marshall, and seems to have no connection to *Kill Bill* beyond the title and the fact that Sommer was a tall (5' 7") blonde.

Time Code: 0:18:24
Information: Music cue, "Ay Que Caray"

Titty bar music, by Marilu Esmeralda Aguiluz.

Time Code: 0:18:24
Information: Image, Budd getting out of his truck, the camera following behind him.

This shot mimics the one of Madsen as Mr. Blonde in *Reservoir Dogs* leaving the hideout to fetch a can of gasoline. Robert Rodriguez used a similar rear tracking shot in *From Dusk Till Dawn*.

Time Code: 0:18:42
Information: Dialogue, "Late again."

Sid Haig makes his obligatory cameo appearance. He was also the judge in *Jackie Brown*, and appeared in several Jack Hill films with Pam Grier, including *Coffy*.

Time Code: 0:19:01
Information: Image, Larry snorting cocaine.

Given his reputation, there are actually very few drugs or drug scenes in Tarantino's movies. *Jackie Brown* is pot addled. *Pulp Fiction* has two drug ingestion scenes, the characters in "The Man From Hollywood" are boozed up, and that's about it. *Pulp Fiction* suggests that there is a hierarchy of drugs, with heroin, the drug of cool jazz musicians, higher than cocaine, a quick rush for the nouveau riche. Larry snorts coke.

Time Code: 0:19:17
Information: "You looking for me?"

The beginning of a lengthy dialogue between Larry and Budd. With their difference in height and weight and the naturalistic acting it can remind the viewer of the great interview scene in Hitchcock's *Psycho* between Martin Balsam as the detective and Anthony Perkins as Norman Bates.

Larry Bishop plays Larry Gomez. He is something of a cult figure to Tarantino.

The son of Rat Pack court jester Joey Bishop and an actor-writer-director in his own right, Bishop, like the son of many a Hollywood dinosaur, entered the exploitation film world in the late

'60s, thus joining near contemporaries such as Peter Fonda and Robert Walker Jr in movies along the lines of *Angels Unchained*. Bishop's threshold crossing into the twilight zone of pulp film was *Wild In The Streets*. His most recent claim to infamy is *Mad Dog Time*, a.k.a., *Trigger Happy*, which appeared on some critics' 10 worst lists of the year in 1996.

Cinematically, aside from appearances in *The Sting II* and *The Big Fix*, not much really was heard from Bishop until 1996, when *Mad Dog Time* appeared briefly in theaters only to be shot down by Roger Ebert. If Bishop's bizarre blend of gangland story and *Cool World* (Gabriel Byrne is in both) is Tarantino- or post-Tarantinoesque, than Tarantino has returned the favor by casting him in *Kill Bill*. There may have been a further influence. The Bride's speech at the end of *Vol. 1* to Sofie Fatale ("I want him to know I know") may have found its roots in dialogue given to the character Jake Parker about 30 minutes into *Mad Dog Time* ("I knew that if I waited, everything could be mine. I waited so long knowing what I knew. Knowing no one else knew what I knew. And I knew that I knew that. I'm one all-knowing fucker").

Mad Dog Time's narrative concerns the return of Vic (Richard Dreyfuss) to rule the unnamed city (think *The King Of New York*, without Walken) that seems to exist only at night and in a dream state, after his brief stay in the nut house. The immediate cause? Grace (Diane Lane, who doesn't show up until the last 10 minutes or so). She's the girlfriend with whom he had an unexplained falling out, though it mostly had to do with Mickey Holliday (Jeff Goldblum), the local roué who has been bedding Grace, along with Rita (Ellen Barkin), his "nighttime" girl, with whom he is reunited after a recent breakup. Rita is also Grace's sister (and their last name is Everly).

Though he is calm, suave, and agreeable, nobody seems to like Mickey much. He particularly inspires vitriol in Ben London (Byrne, here doing a comic, or near-comic, or intentionally comical but in the end rather embarrassing twist on his character of Tom Reagan in *Miller's Crossing*), but Mickey is equally reviled by Jake (Kyle MacLachlan), a rival to Vic, and by Wacky Jacky Jackson (Burt Reynolds).

Now out of the loony bin, Vic intends to sort this all out. He arrives back on the scene to thunderous applause in his club, walking down a red carpet while still in his asylum pajamas, insisting later to Mickey that he has been working with the shrinks on medication that will henceforth chill him out. "Tell Grace it's chemical," he pleads with Mickey. Vic knows that Mickey has been seeing Grace. The one thing keeping Mickey alive is the fact that only Mickey knows where Grace is hiding. The tensions between all the factions come to a head on the night of Vic's second welcome-back party, to which Vic has also invited Nick (Bishop), a renowned hit man, engaged to activate Vic's secret plan.

This all sounds perfectly *noir*ish and gangsterish, but *Mad Dog Time* exists in a weird zone hitherto unknown to film. From its cosmic opening, which serves as visual backdrop to a morbidly intoned philosophical treatise, to its cartoon-like surface, *Mad Dog Time* is less like a movie and more like a graphic novel come to life. It's entrenched in the lore of *noir* and gangster films but also feels a lot like *Dark City* (which Ebert loved, by the way), existing in a dream state beyond logic, like that episode of *Star Trek* in which a whole planet has taken on the mores, lingo, and costumes of 1920s Chicago. One of the irrealities is that citizens of this burg can challenge each other to duels, which are conducted in the spacious basement of a club, the participants sitting behind a desk, with their seconds off to the side. With its tone of kids (i.e., actors) playing grown-up with guns, it's more like *Bugsy Malone* than *Bugsy*.

One could dismiss *Mad Dog Time* as Bishop's cartoony gloss on *Miller's Crossing*, except that there is something fascinatingly gripping about it. I think that the fascination lies in the fact that the film comes across as his bizarre take on the Rat Pack legacy. For one thing, all the songs are by Sinatra, Martin, or Davis. And the cast seems to be constructed along RP lines. Dreyfuss, with his burlap of gray hair, is The Chairman of the Board. Goldblum is Martin, Gregory Hines is Davis. And Byrne, I guess, is Joey, if for no other reason than that he tries to take over Vic's territory via comedy. Dreyfuss, who was a high-school classmate of Bishop's, produced the movie (written about a decade earlier), and other classmates of Bishop's (Rob Reiner) or cronies of the Rat Pack (Henry Silva, Paul Anka) make cameos in the film, along with other oddball integers who help make up one of the most unusual casts in film history, among them Billy Drago, Richard Pryor, Christopher Jones, Michael J. Pollard, Billy Idol, and Juan Fernandez. Bishop reserves for his own character the stage directions, "Smooches with supermodel Angie Everhart in the background."

Bishop's delivery is just as strange here as it is in *Kill Bill*, though not as appealing. He has the habit of putting curse words in sentences in the wrong place. Still, the movie offers further insight into the strange cameo that pops up in the middle of *Kill Bill*.

Not everybody found the film so interesting, however. As mentioned, *Mad Dog Time* has received some of the most scathing reviews ever (though there are pockets of enthusiasm, one of them apparently being Tarantino, who is listed as a cast member in Bishop's next movie).

Time Code: 0:20:20
Information: "That you're as useless as an asshole right here?"

The Rules of Attraction: In Roger Avary's adaptation of the Bret Easton Ellis novel, the character Rupert Guest says, "I need you like I need an asshole on my elbow."

Time Code: 0:20:36
Information: "It's calendar time for Buddy."

This sets a timeline for the film. Larry asks if he is working tomorrow but he isn't, he is working Wednesday. So "today" is Monday, suggesting that The Bride killed Vernita on a Friday, and O-Ren a few days before that.

Time Code: 0:21:28
Information: "And … the hat."

Why does Larry hate hats? Larry is obviously drugged, but there could be deeper reasons than that. Hats are a source of continual fascination and silent communication in John Ford's films, and Larry may be re-emphasizing his "low" state by objecting to Budd's hat, a sign of superiority.

Time Code: 0:22:06
Information: Image, Budd removes his hat.

You feel sorry for Budd. He used to be a well-paid assassin, now he is a drunk and a bouncer, browbeaten by his boss who has no idea what he once was.

Time Code: 0:22:25
Information: Image, Budd's shirt, Southwestern Precision Inc.

There is such a company, in the aeronautics industry. It's located in Gardena, California.

Time Code: 0:22:55 – 00:23:51
Information: Music cue, "A Fistful of Dollars."

By Ennio Morricone, from *Per un Purgano di Dollari*. This music helps us feel for Budd.

Time Code: 0:24:12
Information: Music cue, Johnny Cash's "A Satisfied Mind."

Written by Joe "Red" Hayes and Jack Rhodes. A Johnny Cash song also figures in *Jackie Brown*. In 2000, Tarantino contributed liner notes to a Cash anthology called *Love God Murder*, writing on murder. ""In a country that thinks it's divided by race, where actually, it's divided by economies, Johnny Cash's songs of hillbilly thug life go straight to the heart of the American underclass." He added that, "I've often wondered if gangsta rappers know how little separates their tales of ghetto thug life from Johnny Cash's tales of backwoods thug life. Cash sings tales of men trying to escape – escape the law, escape the poverty they were born into, escape prison, escape madness. But the one thing Cash never lets them escape is regret. Unlike most gangsta rap, Cash's criminal life songs rarely take place during the high times [but] after the cell door has slammed shut or a judge's gavel has condemned a man to death."

The song was first performed by Hayes on an early Starday Records "hillbilly music" anthology. Jean Shepherd, Joan Baez, Graham Parsons, The Byrds (on the *Turn, Turn, Turn* album) and Marty Stewart, are among others who have recorded it. A search of Cash's discography failed to unearth which album Cash performed song.

Time Code: 0:24:15
Information: Image, The Bride reveal.

At the end of a long, dipping crane shot from on high, The Bride is exposed as hiding under Budd's trailer. Tarantino was careful to misdirect us, via shots of Budd looking out on the hills beyond his trailer, and including a POV shot from the mountains.

Time Code: 0:24:56
Information: Image, Budd's boots through the crack of the door.

The "consciousness" of the film has now passed over to The Bride.

Time Code: 0:25:15
Information: Music cue, "Il Mercenario (Ripresa)."

By Ennio Morricone from *Il Mercenario*, as Budd takes off Cash and looks out the window, and after Cash goes back on briefly, this theme emerges for a few moments as The Bride takes off her mask.

Time Code: 0:26:16
Information: Image, Budd in his trailer.

He has changed his shirt. He is also laughing sadistically.

Time Code: 0:26:48
Information: Dialogue, "A double dose of rock salt."

Once again The Bride is prone, on the ground before her attackers.

Time Code: 0:27:07
Information: Dialogue, "Not having tits as fine or as big as yours, I can't imagine how bad that shit must sting."

A hint at some former affection, or at least lust for The Bride?

Time Code: 0:27:34
Information: Image, The Bride spits in Budd's face.

At 00:27:41, Budd spits back, and says "I win" (or "I win?"). Later The Bride uses his chaw tub on Elle.

Time Code: 0:28:01
Information: Image, the needle in The Bride's buttocks.

Budd appears to be a little more prepared for The Bride's visit than his conversation with Bill suggests. Budd is the first of two people to inject The Bride with something, the second being Bill at the end.

Time Code: 0:29:01
Information: Image, Elle Driver.

Note the Band-Aid on her right middle finger. Hannah is missing part of one of her fingers and wears a prosthetic device in public.

Time Code: 0:29:05
Information: Dialogue, "Wrong brother, ya hateful bitch."

Hints of a further backstory. When The Bride left, Bill took up with the more nefarious Elle, who appears to have driven everyone else away.

Time Code: 0:29:21
Information: Sound effect, Elle and Budd talking.

As throughout the film, the sound of their phone conversation is presented as if they were in the same room.

Time Code: 0:29:33
Information: Dialogue, "Anywho."

Like Earl McGraw's "Guestimate," another popular phrase.
The thing about Tarantino's lingo is that it is the kind of talk found on a schoolyard uttered by kids who are trying to act grown

up. "Anywho" is the kind of ersatz-clever variation that someone straining to be clever will resort to. In other words, it's the lingo of aspirants. It is, at its root, uncool. It's what kids straining for a lingo might say, imitating adults.

On the other hand, such phrases communicate clearly.

Time Code: 0:29:58
Information: Dialogue, "Oh, that's hard to say, being that it's … priceless and all."

A sly dig at Bill from their earlier conversation outside Budd's trailer.

Time Code: 0:31:04
Information: Music cue, Charlie Feather's "Can't Hardly Stand It."

Written by Feathers, Jerry Huffman, and Joe Chastain.
The song is playing as Budd and Ernie (Clark Middleton) dig up the grave.

Time Code: 0:31:37
Information: Special effect, the image has reduced to 4x3.

In a sense, the image itself has already put The Bride in a coffin. Also when her consciousness returns the image expands back to its normal size.

Time Code: 0:31:46
Information: Dialogue, "Wakey, wakey. Eggs and bakey."

The catch phrase of band leader Billy Cotton.

Time Code: 0:31:53
Information: Special effect, return to 2.35:1.

Once The Bride is hauled out of the truck bed, the image returns to its former size.

Time Code: 0:32:1508
Information: Image, the headstone of Paula Schultz.

In the spirit of the headstone in John Carpenter's *Halloween*.

Time Code: 0:33:11
Information: Dialogue, "Look at those eyes. This bitch is furious."

Illustrated by a close up of The Bride's eyes, 00:33:12
Spoken by Budd's assistant in crime, Ernie, who represents quite a falling down from Budd's associates in the DiVAS. Between the time he knocked out The Bride and now, Budd had time to find an assistant to help him bury The Bride.

Time Code: 0:33:37
Information: Dialogue, "White women call this 'the silent treatment.' And we let 'em think we don't like it."

Budd doesn't laugh. Earl has just said that he has seen better blondes, but Budd may share his own brother's affinity.

Time Code: 0:34:13
Information: "You're going underneath the ground tonight."

Why does Budd bury The Bride? Why not just shoot her and be done with it? Because first, Elle said she must suffer to her last breath, although, it appears that Budd decided on a "Texas burial" before he called Elle. One could speculate that, unconsciously, Budd does not want to kill The Bride, that he welcomes death and wants to pay his "comeuppance." But it is also a convention in action films that villains select elaborate means of death for heroes, which gives them vast amounts of time to wiggle free.

Time Code: 0:35:14
Information: Dialogue, "Now what's it gonna be, sister?"

The image that goes with this dialogue evokes *Marathon Man* (1976), directed by John Schlesinger from a William Goldman novel, with its choice between dental pain or relief. Here it is flashlight and Mace, though the allusion is probably not intentional.

Budd's holding the Mace close to The Bride's eye comes from Lucio Fulci's *Zombie Flesh Eaters* (1979).

Time Code: 0:35:42
Information: Dialogue, "This is for breaking my brother's heart."

Budd doesn't seem to like his brother, yet is still loyal to him, or at least to his heart. This moment has a faint hint of *The Godfather Part II*, where Michael tells Fredo that he broke his heart.

Time Code: 0:35:49
Information: Image, the screen goes black as the lid of the coffin is put in place. The screen goes black again at 00:36:31.

It's as if the film couldn't bear to show The Bride cry.

Sound effects play an obvious and important role here, and tell the story of what is happening. There is a rumble as she is lowered. Then at 00:37:16 the first thud of dirt as it is shoveled onto her. At 00:37:34 The Bride turns on the flashlight, but the image is black and white, evoking memories of the last time she was prone and in black and white. The sound of the dirt fall grows dimmer as the grave is filled up, and finally we faintly hear the sound of Budd's truck driving away.

The IMDB lists *Gotcha!* (1985) as one of the many films quoted in *Kill Bill*. Aside from a short bedroom scene consisting of dialogue under a black screen I didn't find any resemblances. *Gotcha!* is directed by Jeff Kanew and stars Anthony Edwards as a college kid who stumbles into a spy ring via a love affair with Linda Fiorentino. Tarantino later directed Edwards when he helmed one episode of *ER*.

Time Code: 0:35:55
Information: Dialogue, The Bride begins to whimper.

This is the first time we have seen The Bride "weak."
Time Code: 0:39:15
Information: Title card, "Chapter Eight: The Cruel Tutelage of Pai Mei," with music cue, flute music.

Pai Mei pops up in several Shaw Brothers martial arts films in the '70s and '80s, usually played by Lieh Lo, among them *Hung Hsi-Kuan* (*Shaolin Executioner*, 1977) and *Hung wen tin san po pai lien chiao* (*Fists of the White Lotus*, 1979). There really was a Pai Mei (the name means "White Eyebrow"), and his name is variously Pak Mei (Cantonese) or Bai Mai (Mandarin). Pai Mei was a Wu Dang priest practicing a particularly aggressive style of kung fu who is a villain in Chinese history because he betrayed the southern Shaolin Temple to Manchu tyrants during the Qing Dynasty (1644–1911).

Time Code: 0:39:35
Information: Dialogue, "Once upon a time in China."

An allusion to Tsui Hark's *Once Upon a Time in China* (*Wong Fei-hung*, 1991), its English title coming, obviously, from Leone's film.

As Bill tells the story, he is higher, The Bride lower, looking up, listening, absorbing his wisdom with fascination (or beguiled by his blarney). *Kill Bill* is in large part about the betrayal of mentors, and The Bride first betrays her mentor, Bill, and then is betrayed by him in turn.

Time Code: 0:39:43 – 00:42:08
Information: Dialogue, Bill's Pai Mei story, the Massacre of the Shaolin Temple.

According to Bill, in the year 1003, Pai Mei, head priest of the White Lotus Clan, gives a slight nod to a Shaolin monk but is cut. The next day, Pai Mei visits the Shaolin temple and kills 60 monks. Though narratively coming after, this is chronologically anticipatory of The Bride's handy work in the House of Blue Leaves.

Bill's Pai Mei story is presented like the watch story in *Pulp Fiction*.

Time Code: 0:42:05
Information: Dialogue, "Pai Mei's Five-Point-Palm-Exploding-Heart Technique."

A comical allusion to *Five Fingers Of Death*.

Time Code: 0:42:15
Information: Dialogue, "Did he teach you that?" "No."

The look of interest in The Bride is mirrored in a scene cut out of the film, but included as an extra on the Region 1 DVD. Bill goes on to say that Pai Mei teaches no one the technique.

Time Code: 0:42:24
Information: Dialogue, "If you flash him, even for an instant, a defiant eye, he'll pluck it out."

A set up for the punchline at the end of the Elle Driver thread of the film.

Time Code: 0:44:02
Information: Dialogue, "What happened to you?" "Nothing."

Bill has run into some rough house with Pai Mei. Why? Does Pai Mei also have a grudge against Bill? Does Bill turn against everyone who has mentored him? Bill just says it was "a friendly contest," but appears to have been crucial in convincing Pai Mei to take on The Bride. The moment hints that Pai Mei is the only man who can best Bill in combat.

Time Code: 0:44:49
Information: Dialogue, "When will I see you again?" "That's the title of my favorite soul song of the seventies."

Note how girlish and happy The Bride is. But her "What?" suggests how callow she is and how much she doesn't "get" Bill and his old man's allusions to his own past.

"When Will I See You Again?" was a song by The Three Degrees, a girl group from the '70s, consisting, at that time, of Sheila Ferguson, Valerie Holiday, and Fayette Pinkney.

Time Code: 0:45:36
Information: Image, Bill's license plate, THX 1169.

A salute (of unknown sincerity) to George Lucas, and his science fiction film from 1971 *THX 1138*. Lucas himself, by the way, hides a *THX* reference in all his own movies.

Time Code: 0:45:47 – 00:47:11
Information: Music cue, strumming guitars, probably by Robert Rodriguez.

As the Bride climbs the steps to meet Pai Mei.

Time Code: 0:47:36
Information: Dialogue, The Bride's languages.

She speaks Mandarin and Japanese "very well," but only "a little" Cantonese. This suggests that maybe she was a languages student before Bill spotted her and began his seduction of her into the DiVAS. Note that The Bride is speaking English, while Pai Mei speaks Cantonese, so he clearly understands English. Either that, or it is movie reality. See the section about alternative *Kill Bill*s below.

Time Code: 0:47:51
Information: Image, zoom in on Pai Mei's face.

A common enough visual effect in films by the Shaw Brothers, though some would argue that its roots lie in spaghetti westerns.

Time Code: 0:48:29
Information: Dialogue, "Japanese fat heads."

He later says, "I despise the Goddamn Japs!" (00:49:21). Like Budd, Pai Mei has little regard for others. Also, the Chinese still resent the Japanese for horrific actions during World War II.

Time Code: 0:49:12
Information: Image, Bride standing.

Cinematographer Richardson has captured perfectly that overcast dullness found in Shaw Brothers films.

Time Code: 0:50:25
Information: Image, Pai Mei standing on The Bride's sword blade.

Time Code: 0:50:58
Information: Image, Pai Mei throws the sword aside and it slides into the rack.

This was foreshadowed when Hattori Hanzo threw his sushi knife onto a magnetic rack. The moment also, anticipates some of the tricks in the fight between The Bride and Elle and later, Bill.

Time Code: 0:51:15
Information: Music cue, Isaac Hayes, "Three Tough Guys."

By Isaac Hayes, from the film of the same title.
Time Code: 0:52:10
Information: Dialogue, "Like all Yankee women, all you do
is order in restaurants and spend a man's money."

This is the kind of bitter comment that a guy who didn't
date a lot of women in his nerd years might make after some heady
fame made him "attractive" to women in a high-profile business.

Time Code: 0:52:25
Information: Dialogue, "It's my arm now."

This harks back to The Bride's "owning" the limbs of the fallen in the House of Blue Leaves.

Time Code: 0:53:55 – 00:55:36
Information: Music cue, untitled.

By RZA, as The Bride trains.

Time Code: 0:53:56
Information: Image, The Bride hitting the wood with her fist.

Of all things, this evokes *Karate Kid III* (1989), in which an evil mentor tricks the Kid into training by hitting wood columns with his fists. Pai Mei says at 00:54:19 saying, "It is the wood that should fear your hand, not the other way around," and "You acquiesce to defeat," much in the spirit of training advice in kung fu movies.

Time Code: 0:54:43
Information: Image, training montage.

Amid all the images (The Bride trudging up the stairs, shot with a zoom; board work; sleeping and hitting the wall in her sleep, and the eating chopsticks scene) there are two images, of The Bride silhouetted against a red backdrop, and then doing moves in unison with Pai Mei. This is another allusion to *Samurai Fiction*.

Time Code: 0:57:23 – 01:04:59
Information: Music cue, "Il Mercenario (Ripresa)."

By Ennio Morricone from *Il Mercenario*, as the film returns to The Bride in the coffin, 00:57:44.

Time Code: 01:01:30
Information: Image, The Bride breaks through the wood, dirt falls in, and she rises to the surface.

This is the scene that seems the most impossible to fans wavering in their appreciation of the film. Pai Mei leaping onto The Bride's blade is OK to them, but this …

The moment has several fathers. One is Lucio Fulci's *Paura nella città dei morti viventi* (*The Gates of Hell*, *City of the Living Dead*, 1980), in which a woman is buried alive, and then manages to get to the surface (the *Kill Bill* script makes this reference explicit) Another is *The Matrix* (1999), when the virtual warriors hide in the walls of a building to escape capture. The whole buried alive situation also reminds viewers of *The Vanishing* (*Spoorloos*, 1988), and its later American remake (1993).

Another source might be "Final Escape," an episode from the next-to-last season of *Alfred Hitchcock Presents*, starring Edd Byrnes as a work-farm convict attempting a tricky escape, or Sam Peckinpah's *Bring Me the Head of Alfredo Garcia* (1974).

Finally, *Lone Wolf McQuade* (1983), one of the better Chuck Norris films, seems a likely antecedent, although in that film Norris is buried alive in his truck. David Carradine also stars in *Lone Wolf McQuade*.

Time Code: 01:01:54
Information: Image, The Bride's hand coming out of the grave.

An obvious reference to Brian De Palma's *Carrie* (1976), based on the Stephen King novel. In a dream sequence at the end of the film, Carrie's hand comes out of the grave and grabs the wrist of the Sue Snell character. De Palma, in turn, got the effect from the end of John Boorman's *Deliverance* (1972), where a guilt-haunted Jon Voight dreams of the hand of a corpse popping out of the water and exposing his crimes. But hands through graveyard dirt are a common enough trick.

Time Code: 01:02:3043
Information: Image, the risen from the grave gag.

A diner resides across the street from the graveyard, and The Bride crosses the street with a cloud of dust trailing her. Inside she asks for a glass of water. Forum posters have likened this image to Charles Schulz's cartoon character Pigpen, and cite it as the second allusion to *Peanuts* in the movie.

Time Code: 01:03:06
Information: Title card, "Chapter Nine: Elle and I."

When I first saw this I wondered, shouldn't it be "me"? But experts inform me that both work in this context. In any case, this locution foreshadows a visual punch line: Elle and eye.

Time Code: 01:03:06 – 01:01:04
Information: Music cue, "The Chase."

"The Chase" was composed by Alan Reeves, Phil Steele,, and Philip Brigham, for the 1971 film *Road to Salina*.

Road to Salina is a not-uninteresting nexus of styles and intentions. Directed by Georges Lautner from his own script, it blends the hippie ethos of the late '60s (world traveling, sexual liberation) with the psychosis of the older oppressive generations, and the crime premises of James Cain. The plot has young Jonas (Robert Walker, Jr.) hitchhiking through Spain and stopping at the roadside cafe of Mara (Rita Hayworth). She instantly mistakes him for her long-lost son Rocky (played in a flashback by Marc Porel), who disappeared four years earlier. Jonas gladly accepts the role of son, at first just for a few minutes so that he can get a meal and something to drink, but later for the long term, after he meets Mara's other child, her daughter Billie (Mimsy Farmer). Though Billie pretends that Jonas is Rocky, both she and Mara's friend Warren (Ed Begley) know that he is not. Warren accepts his presence on the premises because he has made Mara happy for the first time since Rocky fled. Billie accepts him because through Jonas she can re-create the incestuous longings she experienced with her brother. There's also a bit of *The Return of Martin Guerre* in the film.

The film begins in the rain, as Jonas flees the cafe. He makes his way to the police station, where he begins to tell his story as the officer accompanies him back to Mara's. The bulk of the film is Jonas's chronologically told flashback. Director Launtner opens the film in the rain, but the rest of *Salina* takes place in oppressive heat.

Billie drives a yellow convertible, and the music cue "The Chase" is used a couple of times to accompany her driving. *Kill Bill* also uses "Sunny Road to Salina," from the film, written by Daniel Bevilacqua and performed by the French pop star Christophe.

It's unclear if Tarantino has actually seen *Road To Salina*. Apparently the musical cue was suggested to him by Julia Dreyfus. If he hasn't seen it, he might like it. Billie drives a yellow American convertible as she tears through the desert. Farmer is an interesting actress, from the "crazy" and fragile school that includes Rosanna Arquette, and Jean Seberg. Farmer is pixieish, but she with aggressive teeth, like Tippy Walker in *The World of Henry Orient*, and her lower lip is completely out of control. The desert scenes have the accusatory isolation of Antonioni's *Zabriskie Point*.

Unfortunately, as of this writing the film is only available in a pan-and-scan VHS tape.

Time Code: 01:03:20
Information: Image, Elle's car, a Pontiac Firebird.

Apparently, this is Daryl Hannah's own vehicle. It's also the car that Burt Reynolds drives in *Smokey And The Bandit* (1977).

Time Code: 01:03:58
Information: Image, Elle walking to the trailer, with a red bag.

Another sly allusion to *Marnie*, in which Tippi Hedren's Marnie is shown walking away from the camera carrying a bag.

Elle's black pantsuit is the same one Jackie Brown buys in the mall, a Jones New York suit, and the same one Mia Wallace wears in *Pulp Fiction*. It's also similar to the suit Isabelle Adjani wears in Walter Hill's *The Driver* (1978).

Time Code: 01:04:04
Information: Image, shock cut to the sun, straight on, rings of the lens, then dissolve to The Bride walking.

Some writers have said that this is derived from *Once Upon A Time In The West*, that is, the shots of Henry Fonda's Frank walking into focus in Harmonica's memories. It's also an allusion to Clint Eastwood's appearance in *High Plains Drifter* (1973). The shot is continued or reiterated at 01:04:55.

Time Code: 01:04:09 – 010528
Information: Music cue, "Sunny Road to Salina?"

By Christophe, also from *Road To Salina*, as The Bride walks through the desert.

Time Code: 01:05:12
Information: Image, The Bride on the ridge, looking down at Budd's trailer as Elle arrives.

This has been likened to Jason Robards looking down on Charles Bronson as he takes out a few of Henry Fonda's men in *Once Upon A Time In The West*.

Time Code: 01:05:28 – 01:05:59
Information: Music cue, *Ironside* theme.

From a close up, The Bride who runs off camera right, in a very effective shot.

Time Code: 01:04:55
Information: Dialogue, "So that's a Texas funeral."

The phrase does not occur in *Texas Crude*, Ken Weaver's compendium of Texasisms.

Time Code: 01:05:51
Information: Image, Elle pulls out a pad.

There is something very funny and graceful about the way Hannah repeatedly yanks out her pad and flips open the top.

Time Code: 01:06:21
Information: Image, overhead shot of tequila pouring.

A favorite Tarantino shot, derived, as noted before, from Godard, Scorsese, and Van Sant.

Time Code: 01:06:31
Information: Sound effect, the sound of the blender whirling with the ting of the glade, and Elle's comment obscured.

Almost every second of *Kill Bill* has been put under the virtual microscope in cyberspace. The Tarantino Archive forum even has a section on the meaning of this scene. The conclusion the posters came to was that it added to the film's verisimilitude – this really happens in real life, people's words obscured by noise. Something similar happens in *Jackie Brown* when Max Cherry comes by her apartment the next morning to pick up his gun.

Time Code: 01:06:36
Information: Image, Budd's shirt, Quality Store.

Unknown. One of several mysterious shirts in the film.

Time Code: 01:06:58
Information: Dialogue, Budd's irritation with Elle over comparing swords.

Budd has managed to be civil to the "hateful bitch," but some vestige of his DiVAS pride erupts when this relative newbie reveals that she doesn't know how to judge a Hanzo sword.

Time Code: 01:07:25
Information: Dialogue, "Wrap your lips around that."

Another colloquialism.

Time Code: 01:07:37 – 01:08:15
Information: Dialogue, "Which 'R' are you filled with?," and the retirement discussion.

The theme of work pops up again. For a fuller discussion of this topic, I direct the reader shamelessly to my Pocket Essentials book on Tarantino.

Time Code: 01:08:21
Information: Image, *Mr. Majestyk* poster.

Seen on the wall of the trailer behind Budd. *Mr. Majestyk* (1974), directed by Richard Fleischer, is based on an Elmore Leonard script, which he later turned into a novel.

As mentioned before, there is a Charles Bronson reference in every Tarantino film.

Time Code: 01:08:26
Information: Dialogue, "Relief or regret?"

On the liner notes for the Johnny Cash anthology *Love God Murder*, Tarantino writes, ""When a man faces a rope or 99 years in a cage for the choices he made, when he tells the story of those choices, he tells it not with bravado, but an overwhelming sense of regret.""

Time Code: 01:08:57
Information: Dialogue, "I never saw anyone buffalo Bill the way she buffaloed Bill."

Had he eyes a worse buffaloer is standing before him in the shape of Elle Driver, as we are about to learn.

Time Code: 01:09:06
Information: Dialogue, "I tried to tell him, she was just smart for a blonde."

A vague dig at Elle, and an allusion to the "blonde jokes" that were so popular in the 1980s.

Time Code: 01:09:12
Information: Image, overhead shot of Budd opening the red suitcase.

Another insert derived from Godard, Scorsese, and specifically, Gus Van Sant, in *Drugstore Cowboy* (1989).

Time Code: 01:09:5519
Information: Image, Budd seeing the money.

Michael Madsen's laugh here is exquisite.

Time Code: 01:09:29
Information: Image, Elle chewing the ice.

Probably not intentional, but this moment reminded me of Alec Baldwin chewing the ice in *Malice* (1993).

Time Code: 01:09:42
Information: Image, the black mamba in the suitcase.

The snake bites Budd thrice, in the face.

Time Code: 01:10:30
Information: Dialogue, "I looked him up on the Internet."

This may be an in-joke. Tarantino is reputedly computer-phobic. Which is one reason why, in August 2004, fans were skeptical when a Tarantino blog suddenly emerged on the World Wide Web. Most posters thought it was a hoax, but some were taken in by it (including this author).

Time Code: 01:11:26
Information: Dialogue, "Now you should listen to this, 'cause it concerns you."

Ordell says the same thing in *Jackie Brown*.

Time Code: 01:11:34
Information: Dialogue, "Gargantuan."

One of the best lines in the movie, well-delivered by Hannah.

Time Code: 01:11:45
Information: Dialogue about anti-venom.

A Black Mamba figures in the thriller *Venom* (1982) with Klaus Kinski and Oliver Reed .

Time Code: 01:12:26
Information: Dialogue, "Regret, that maybe the greatest warrior I have ever met her end at the hands of a bushwackin', scrub, alky piece of shit like you."

A fairly accurate summary of Budd.

Time Code: 01:12:52
Information: Music cue, untitled by probably by Rodriguez.

As Elle cleans up the trailer.

Time Code: 01:13:23
Information: Image, Elle pulls out her cell phone.

It's Bill. She lies to him and says that The Bride killed Budd with a Black Mamba, but that she killed The Bride. In other words, she lies and cheats and doesn't follow a warrior's code.

Time Code: 01:14:03
Information: Dialogue, "Huntington cemetery on Fuller and Guadalupe."

An allusion to Samuel Fuller (1911 – 1997), the director of gritty classics in a wide variety of modes and genres. He's most famous for *Pickup on South Street* (1953), *Forty Guns* (1957), and *Shock Corridor*(1963), and was a true writer-director. Godard honored him by giving Fuller a cameo in *Pierrot le fou* (1965). Tarantino appears in an IFC channel documentary about Fuller, *The Typewriter, The Rifle And The Movie Camera* (1996). The reverend that Harvey Keitel plays in *From Dusk Till Dawn* is also named Fuller.

Time Code: 01:14:08
Information: Dialogue, "You will be standing at the final

resting place of Beatrix Kiddo."

Elle is the first person allowed to say The Bride's real name unbleeped.

Time Code: 01:14:13
Information: Dialogue, "Marty Kitrosser?"

Martin Kitrosser has worked as script supervisor on all of Tarantino's movies. He has also written and starred in several of the *Friday the 13th* movies, and is credited with coming up with the hockey mask idea. He wrote and directed *Silent Night, Deadly Night 5: The Toy Maker* (1992)

Time Code: 01:14:14
Information: Dialogue, "Melanie Harrhouse?"

Unknown.

Time Code: 01:14:18
Information: Image, The Bride saying "Here"

The Bride is shown with braces and wearing her tan leather burial coat.
The moment is likened to a similar current self in childhood classroom setting in Woody Allen's *Annie Hall*, but it could just as easily come from Adam Sandler's *Billy Madison* (1995), Tarantino being a fan of the comedian.

Time Code: 01:14:52
Information: Image, The Bride whips Elle with the TV antenna.

Close fights in tight spaces occur in the James Bond film *From Russia With Love* (1963) and The Coen brothers' *Raising Arizona* (1987), which also takes place in a trailer. Other sources might be the fight between Frank Sinatra and Henry Silva in *The Manchurian Candidate* (1962), and the brawl in the bathroom in Walter Hill's *The Warriors* (1979).
Surprisingly, *Jackass: The Movie* (2002) was also an

influence. It apparently inspired him to dirty up the trailer brawl between the two blonde Gargantuans. "Oh, he just loves *Jackass*. Much to my chagrin," Thurman told *Maxim* magazine.

Time Code: 01:15:18
Information: Image, the duo knock each other down and the image separates into split screen.

Reminiscent of Roger Avary's *The Rules of Attraction* (2002) when stars James Van Der Beek and Shannyn Sossamon meet in a hallway, each followed by one half of a split screen.

Time Code: 01:15:38
Information: Image, Budd's spit can.

The label is Oak Ridge Coffee, which is made near Tarantino's birthplace in Kentucky.

Time Code: 01:15:57
Information: Sound effect, as Elle falls over the counter onto a guitar.

The twang you hear comes from the Hanna-Barbera cartoon sound effects catalog, another example of numerous moments in the film using comical sound effects derived from cartoons or kung fu movies.

Time Code: 01:16:25
Information: Image, Elle's head in the toilet.

This moment could be from *Trainspotting*'s famous scene where Ewan McGregor falls into the toilet, but most likely comes from a similar scene in Jack Hill's *Switchblade Sisters*.

Time Code: 01:17:00
Information: Image, shock zoom into The Bride's eyes as she sees Budd's Hattori Hanzo sword.

A nice moment.

Time Code: 01:17:05
Information: Dialogue, "To my brother Budd. The only man I ever loved. Bill."

Is the real love story here between Bill and Budd?
I love the way The Bride perkily says "Bill" as she snaps the blade back into its sheath and rises to do battle.

Time Code: 01:17:13
Information: Music cue, Morricone, music from the start.

Reprise of "Silhouette of Doom."

Time Code: 01:17:42
Information: Dialogue, "Elle." "Bea."

There are a lot of "letter" names in *Kill Bill*: Elle (L), Bea (B), plus O-Ren (and Air-O), and B. B. The script also had a character called J. T.

Time Code: 01:17:58
Information: Dialogue, "I called him a miserable old fool."

"Miserable Old Fool" doesn't seem all that insulting, but in the touchy world of martial arts masters, who knows?

Time Code: 01:18:06
Information: Dialogue, "I killed that miserable old fool."

Killing a character's master is a common trope in martial arts films. In the deleted scene that appears on the Region 1 DVD, Bill is accosted in a market by a man whose master he has killed.

Time Code: 01:18:39
Information: Image, Elle standing over Pai Mei

Elle stands over Pai Mei with the same relish Santanico Pandemonium stands over Seth Gecko in *From Dusk Till Dawn*.

Time Code: 1:19:04
Information: Dialogue, "Bitch, you don't have a future."

One of those great movie movie lines. It probably has a few antecedents, but let's just enjoy it here for Thurman's delivery.

Time Code: 1:19:49
Information: The Bride plucks out Elle's eye.

This was not in the script. It's a clever summation of the eye themes of the movie and an ingenious variation on the battle as it is found in the screenplay.

There are lots of blindings in the movies that Tarantino favors. The evil witch in *Iron Monkey* is blinded in one eye just before she dies. Lucio Fulci's films are also filled with outrages against vulnerable eyeballs. Key eyeball massacre scenes occur in Fulci's *Zombie Flesh Eaters* (1979) and *The Beyond* (1981). A character is blinded in *Coffy.*

Time Code: 1:19:54
Information: Image, Elle writhing on the bathroom floor.

A mini-homage to the character Hannah played, Pris, in *Blade Runner*. Her thrashing around may also have been influenced by a similar scene near the end of *Last House On The Left.*

Time Code: 1:21:12
Information: Title card, "Last Chapter: Face to Face"
In keeping with the theme of using movie titles or near titles, this one echoes the Bergman film, not for any particular reason, however.

The chronological order of the titles is as follows:

Chapter 3: The Origin of O-Ren

Chapter 8: The cruel tutelage of Pai Mei.

The Lisa Wong Hit.

Chapter 6: Massacre at Two Pines.

Chapter 2: The Blood-Splattered Bride (when The Bride is comatose).

Queen of the Crime Council (O-Ren rise to power).

Chapter 2: The Blood-Splattered Bride (the second half).
Chapter 4: The Man from Okinawa
Chapter 5: Show Down at House of Blue Leaves
Bill visits Budd.
Chapter 1: Two
Chapter 7: The Lonely Grave of Paula Schultz
Chapter 9: Elle and I
Chapter 10: Face to Face

Time Code: 1:21:19
Information: Music cue, "Tu Mira"

Choral music for the panorama of Mexico at sunset, by Lole Y Manuel.

Time Code: 1:21:41
Information: The Bride's car.

Bride blasts into view in a robin's egg blue Karmann Ghia. Does the change in color from red to blue symbolize a change in The Bride's resolve? Or is it just another cool car that Tarantino likes.

Time Code: 1:21:05
Information: The Bride arrives to meet Esteban at El Botanero Cochon.

This scene is supposed to take place in Acuna, Mexico. Acuna is the city in which Robert Rodriguez's *El Mariachi* takes place. Shooting took place at Punta Careyes, on the west coast of Mexico in the second week of February of 2003. The Bride's conversation with Esteban comprises the last scenes Thurman shot for the film. This setting appeared in stories about the movie in *Entertainment Weekly* and elsewhere, indicating that the prostitutes lounging in the background are all real. "We made a location in Francisco Villa, in a bar (el Botanero Cochon), only with extras that were not professionals," Benjamin Suarez, a location coordinator, told a Mexican paper. "There were some sluts, the place was really depressing. When we got there it was a dump, but Tarantino decided that it should be there." The article was by Hector Contreras for Agencia Reforma.

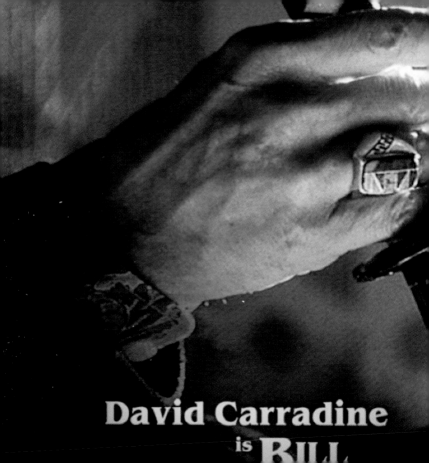

David Carradine is BILL

THE NEW FILM BY QUENTIN TARANTINO

APRIL 16, 2004

DEATH   LIST FIVE

①O-REN   ~~ISHII~~

②~~VERNITA GREEN~~

③BUDD

④ELLE DRIVER

⑤BILL

KILL BILL

VOL.2

謀殺比雨

hurman
THE BRIDE

THE DEADLY VIPER A

BLACK MAMBA

COPPERHEAD

CALIFORNIA MOUNTAIN SNAKE

THE 4TH FILM BY QUENTIN TA

KILL

ASSINATION SQUAD

SIDEWINDER

COTTONMOUTH

BILL

KILL 謀殺吐爾 BILL
VOL.2

Observers have likened this passage in the movie to *Apocalypse Now* (1979), with The Bride, near the end of her bloody journey, like Willard facing Kurrz. There is even an ox in the background, a tag from *AN*. The shot of the trees The Bride is passing have the flavor of the trees in *AN*.

El Botanero Cochon translates, very roughly, as "pig bar." According to Susan Dearing at www.gomanzanillo.com/features/botaneros, "a botana is a free snack, usually given out in bars or botaneros, where, as tradition dictates, as long as you keep drinking, the food is free."

Time Code: 1:22:18
Information: Dialogue, "Like most men who never knew their fathers, Bill collected father figures."

This applies equally to Tarantino, who has had a succession of father substitutes in his life.

Here's what we know about Esteban Vihaio. He ran a brothel in Acuna for 50 years and was a friend of Bill's mother. He is 80, retired, and once ran the Acuna Boys, the gang made up of the offspring of his whores, Bill being one of them (along with Budd?).

Time Code: 1:23:16
Information:
The book Esteban is reading. *The Carrucan's of Kurrajong*, by Jasmine Yuen.

The book must have some significance, given that Tarantino holds a close up of it. Or it may just be action filler, like the fender of a car as someone is driving it.

But let's assume that the book does have significance. There is a kangaroo on the cover, which makes the book at first appear to be some kind of travel account. But the possessive on Carrucan suggests that in fact it is a family genealogy. Most genealogies are privately published and look not unlike this book. Of course, there is always the chance that the possessive is simply a typo by a set designer, but in any case if it is intentional it is funny that Vihaio is reading a genealogical account (of his own family?) given that the movie is so preoccupied with family matters.

Kurrajong is a village west of Sidney, Australia in the Great

Dividing Range, on the way to Lithgow. The place is famous for its baked meat pies. Remember that The Bride quickly manufactures an Australian silver mining enterprise for Bill when he meets Tommy.

Jasmine Yuen-Carrucan appears in the credits twice, as a production assistant, and as Second Assistant Camera.

Also on the table is a copy of the *Wall Street Journal*. Thus the message is given that Vihaio, in his eighth decade is, and continues to be, a man of culture and business acumen.

Time Code: 1:23:41
Information: **Dialogue**, "I must warn you I am most susceptible to flattery."

Critically, what must be noted here is the absolute brilliance of Parks as Vihaio.

Time Code: 1:24:18
Information: Dialogue, Vihaio tells of taking Bill to see a Lana Turner movie at the age of five.

Thus the birth of Bill's fixation on blondes. Vihaio calls him a "fool for blondes." The "blondest" Lana Turner movie is *The Postman Always Rings Twice*. *Postman* was released in 1946. If Bill were roughly the same age as David Carradine – 67 – then he would have seen the film when he was 10. Bear in mind that *Road to Salina* also resembles *Postman*.

This passage is also autobiographical. Tarantino's stepfathers, first Curtis Zastoupil and later Jan Bohusch both took Tarantino to lots of movies.

Time Code: 01:24:45
Information: Dialogue, "Fool for blondes."

Tarantino used the song "Fool for Love" in *Reservoir Dogs*.

Time Code: 1:25:22
Information: Vihaio notices that The Bride is not driving a truck.

Vihaio has had conversations with someone, presumably

Bill, about The Bride. "My pussy Wagon died on me," The Bride says, in a remnant of a section deleted from the script, Yuki's Revenge, in which the Pussy Wagon is destroyed.

> **Time Code**: 1:25:46
> **Information:** Vihaio says, "I would have just cut your face."

This is the set up for the visual gag that is about to follow. As mentioned ad nauseam, most of the gags in *KB* are visual.

> **Time Code**: 01:26:09
> **Information:** Dialogue, "Dos Anjeho."

Anjeho is a potent brand of rum that was popular with the kids in the late 1970s to early 1980s.

> **Time Code**: 1:26:20
> **Information:** Shot of Clara with her disfigured face.

So this is instant example of Vihaio's approach to betrayal. In the twilight moments of the movie, Bill is contrasted with his mentor, who, it should be noted, survives the film.

Bill clearly has taken after his father figure, starting his own "team," smaller but more global and profitable.

> **Time Code**: 1:26:53
> **Information:** "Bill's at the Villa Quatro, on the road to Salina."

Why does Vihaio "give up" Bill so easily? He asks The Bride if she is wondering that same thing. She says no, but he tells her anyway – that Bill would want him to tell her where he is. The Bride allows as how she doesn't believe him." How else is he ever going to see you again," 01:27:18 referring back to the '70s soul tune Bill likes.

The moment also provides another nod to the film *Road to Salina*, from which Tarantino derived the car driving music for the driving Elle.

Quatro might be an allusion to rocker Suzi Quatro, who played Leather Tuscadero, sister to Pinky Tuscadero, on *Happy Days*.

Time Code: 1:27:26

Information: Image, dissolve to black and white footage of the road from the POV of The Bride driving, approaching the Villa Quatro.

The black and white used here matches that used at the end of *Vol. 1*'s "sneak preview" of *Vol. 2*.

Time Code: 01:27:20

Information: Music cue, "Summertime Killer."

By Luis Bacalov, from the movie *Motorcycle Circus*, which plays through The Bride's entrance into Bill's apartment.

Time Code: 1:27:27

Information: Image, the Bride's Hattori Hanzo sword.

In color, against the black and white backdrop of the rear projection, followed the profile of the car's front end, and The Bride's profile. This rhymes with the swords in its seat holder on the Air-O plane.

Time Code: 1:27:45

Information: Image, montage of The Bride entering the Villa.

The main point communicated is through the look of pleased anticipation on The Bride's face.

Also notable that neither the car guy nor the desk people bother The Bride about her sword, a convention within the world of *Kill Bill*. Tarantino talks in an interview about how Warren Beatty didn't get the whole sword carrying aspect of the movie, unable to grok its alternative universe – Bizarro world aspect.

The Villa Quatro is obviously a large complex not unlike a residence inn, catering to rich people.

Producer Lawrence Bender is one of the hotel clerks in the background, 01:27:48

Time Code: 1:27:55
Information: Bill's room number, 101.

This is the same room number on Neo's door in *The Matrix*, but also the terrifying torture chamber in George Orwell's *1984*. That where the forces of oppression break you by confronting you with your worst fear (in Winston Smith's case, rats). This may be an echo of Bill's opening talking about his sadism versus masochism. Room 101 is a dream room for readers of magazines such as *Drummer*.

Time Code: 1:28:25 – 01:28:28
Information: Music Cue, "Invincible Pole Fighter."

The music is old, and even sounds mono and shredded. It's from a Shaw brothers movie, followed by "The Demise Of Barbara and the Return of Joe," from *Navaho Joe*.

Time Code: 1:28:27
Information: Bill and B. B. playing guns.

Obviously, Vihaio has told Bill that The Bride was coming. Bill in turn has told his daughter that her mother is coming. Bill then arranges this comically ironic playtime tableaux of gunplay.

The main thing that this sequence does is draw upon the credit sequence song for part one, Nancy Sinatra's rendition of "Bang Bang," the Cher song written by Sonny Bono.

Time Code: 1:28:35
Information: Close up of The Bride and her shifting emotions.

Anyone who is a fan of *Alias* will note that The Bride is called upon to express numerous emotions, often-contradictory ones in the same scene or shot.

Time Code: 1:28:56
Information: Image, Bill and B.B. prone.

A variation on The Bride's being on the ground.

Time Code: 1:29:54
Information: The Bride collapsing.
The Bride has quickly adapted herself to the game. Quick adaptation of a character or pose is a part of being cool. And a running theme in Tarantino's work is acting.

Time Code: 1:30:45
Information: Dialogue, "Because Mommy's been dreaming of you."

Bill had a dream before he shot her, though he never tells us what it was.

Time Code: 1:30:57
Information: Music cue, "The Return of Joe, by Morricone.

Underscores her resolved to still get revenge.

Time Code: 1:32:11
Information: Dialogue, "B. B., don't you think mommy has the prettiest hair in the whole wide world?"

Bill's hair fetish, mentioned by Vihaio, is affirmed.

Time Code: 1:32:09
Information: Image, Bill starting to make the sandwich.

This scene rhymes with the opening fight between The Bride and Vernita, who pause in mid-battle to get coffee.
"Bimbo Bread," the brand name of the loaf that Bill is using to make his daughter a sandwich, is of course fake.

Time Code: 1:32:49
Information: Dialogue, the story about Emilio the goldfish.

Viewers will recall that The Bride stepped on Elle Driver's eye after she plucked it out.
At 01:34:49, Bill says, "Is that not the perfect visual image of life and death?"

Time Code: 1:35:38
Information: Dialogue, "What I didn't know was, when I shot Mommy, what would happen to me."

Bill goes on to say that it made him sad, to do such a thing that he couldn't undo. Presumably this is his first experience with sadness.
Question: Was Elle young B. B.'s foster mother?
Bill seems to think that he will get a reprieve from death by using the B. B. card, but it didn't work for Vernita.

Time Code: 1:36:51
Information: Dialogue, B. B. wants to watch *Shogun Assassin* with The Bride.

Shogun Assassin is a conflation by Roger Corman's New World Pictures conflation of three films from the Lone Wolf and Cub series, *Lone Wolf and Cub: Sword of Vengeance*, *Lone Wolf and Cub: Baby Cart at the River Styx*, *Lone Wolf and Cub: Baby Cart to Hades*, all from 1972, and directed by Kenji Masume. The Lone Wolf and Cub films are themselves adapted from a long series of *manga*. Tony Mustafa writes that "The Lone Wolf and Cub films totally reconstructs the Samurai genre—they are so different from the traditional, honorable Samurai epics like the Zatoichi series. The dark cinematic world of Lone Wolf is graphically violent, and owes more to the Spaghetti Western than it does to the Akira Kurosawa Samurai classics."

At the end of *Kill Bill*, a title will read that the lion is back with her cub.

Time Code: 01:37:34
Information: Dialogue, from *Shogun Assassin*, "When he would see her, he would forget about the killings."

Perhaps this is what Bill hopes.

Time Code: 01:37:45
Information: Music cue, "About Her," Malcolm McLaren.

A sampling by the fabled punk rock producer and promoter.

Time Code: 01:40:07
Information: Image, Bride walking down the lighted hallway.

A common enough mage, but not unlike a similar scene in Fellini's *City of Women*. I doubt if there is a connection, however.

Time Code: 01:40:44
Information: Image, William Witney's *The Golden Stallion*

on the television in Bill's living room. There is a close up of Roy Rogers at 01:41:21

During his long hiatus between films, Tarantino, as is his wont, spent a lot of time watching films. And not just watching them, but studying them, sifting through them in search of clues about the art of cinema, and looking for *auteurs* that could speak to him whom nobody else was celebrating. He came up with his own personal pantheon of favorite filmmakers, one not unlike the ranking of directors that Andrew Sarris devised in his book *The American Cinema*, with the difference that helmers whom Sarris might have consigned to his category Expressive Esoterica QT would put in the Pantheon. William Witney is one of them, and he had a long career in films.

On Friday, September 15, 2000, to usher in a new century and to commence a new, if irregular and short-lived, series in the *New York Times*, reporter Rick Lyman sat down with the loquacious Tarantino to interview him about movies.

Lyman's goal for the series was to talk with a prominent filmmaker while watching a favorite movie with them. Usually, but not always, the filmmaker was promoting a new release. Tarantino, on the other hand, was not. In fact, he hadn't made a film since *Jackie Brown* in 1997. Tarantino didn't want to talk about his latest movie, his career, or his interesting past. He wanted to talk about William Witney.

Tarantino had been wading through the vast wealth of pulp films of the middle 20th century. And there, amid the unyielding pabulum of America's commercial empire, he made a discovery: director William Witney, who worked for Republic pictures most of his life and is most famous, if at all, for making a bunch of Roy Rogers westerns in the '40s.

Witney got into the movie biz the old fashioned way: he knew somebody. His brother in law was already a director of serials at Mascot, a Saturday afternoon serial manufacturing company later absorbed into Republic. During a summer break from studying for his Annapolis entrance exams, Witney subbed for a while as a stunt man and horse rider for some quickly made western serials.

To his surprise, Witney later failed his Annapolis exams, and, returning to work with his brother-in-law, never left. He learned movies from the ground up: props, stunts, editing, handling the camera, and later even writing. By the time he started directing, in his early 20s (at first just stepping in for a drunk director sent home from the set), he had had thorough and priceless film training.

Born in Oklahoma and raised near San Diego, Witney was an animal lover, and his films are touched by a reverence for and an understanding of all manner of creatures — even human beings.

In the TIMES, Tarantino offers a sympathetic account of one of Witney's best Roy Rogers films, *The Golden Stallion,* originally released in 1949 and one of Tarantino's favorites. In particular, Tarantino points out how unexpectedly *weird* the movie is, countering to our expectations of what we might think a Roy Rogers movie is supposed to be like. For one thing, Rogers's character goes to jail for five years for a crime he doesn't commit in order to spare his horse Trigger from summary judgment. As Rogers grapples with his decision to take the fall for his horse, Witney's camera tracks in slowly on his Eastmancolored face. It's a breathtaking and powerful moment, and utterly unexpectedly stylish. Witney had in fact been summoned to "save" the Rogers series of westerns. He dressed Rogers down in more conventional garb (no more bejeweled blouses) and orchestrated brutal fight scenes for the dandified star.

Tarantino makes out Witney to sound like a fascinating guy, among other things as the inventor of "choreographed" fight scenes, among many other action techniques still used in commercial Hollywood cinema. "I've found directors I like, but William Witney is ahead of them all. I think it's so cool that he began as the king of cowboy serials and ended with a black exploitation film," he told Lyman. "That's a career, man." In June of 2001 Tarantino joined a panel at the Seattle film festival to discuss Witney, showing several of his films, including *Stranger At My Door*, *Eyes Of Texas*, *The Outcast*, *The Bonnie Parker Story*, *Paratrooper Command*, *Juvenile Jungle*, and *Santa Fe Passage*, conducting what he called a tutorial on Witney.

And every August Tarantino carts his own prints of beloved films to Austin for his a 10-day festival, where he often touts Witney's work (along with films such as *Dark Of The Sun*, *Dixie Dynamite* and *Billy Jack*). Surprisingly, Witney was still alive when Tarantino first started praising him. But he died at the age of 86 in March of 2002 in a nursing home in the Sierra Nevadas. His obits noted that he directed anywhere from 60 and to 100 films.

Witney's own views on himself are compile in his fascinating insider's autobiography, *In A Door, Into A Fight, Out A*

Door, Into A Chase, a charming account of the first half of his life, taking him onto the brink of his service in WWII. It's a Hollywood memoir that appears to be *actually written* by Witney himself.

Witney's book evokes a time when, in Poverty Row studios, movies were made for the love of the blossoming art and for the engagement in commercial storytelling. Witney reveals a lot about how the art of cinema evolved. He identifies the man who invented the shooting schedule (page 22). He describes what it was like to work with Bela Lugosi, whom he directed in Saturday afternoon serials. He explains how he invented the modern cinematic fist fight. And Witney is also frank about the hardships of moviemaking, and dishes a little dirt about certain drunks and fakes.

All of William Witney's movies are probably trivial to most people who consider themselves sophisticated film aficionados. But Witney's films show an energy and craft that is deeply gratifying. And in the end, amid the onslaught of pumped up vacuities that vie for our mania, there is only craft, and its small pleasures.

Time Code: 01:41:21
Information: Dialogue, "It just so happens this hacienda has its own private beach."

A scene at the beach, a final confrontation between Bill and The Bride, was included in the screenplay, but dropped from the movie for budgetary reasons.

Time Code: 01:41:51
Information: Image, The Bride eyeing Bills sword atop the TV.

This comes from the start of *Death Rides a Horse*, in which the father of the family about to be slaughtered glances at the rifle he wants to seize in order to ward off the intruders.

Time Code: 01:42:03
Information: Dialogue, "Now if you don't settle down, I'm gonna have to put one in your kneecap. And I hear tell that's a very painful place to get shot in."

Similar analyses appear in *Reservoir Dogs* and *Jackie*

Brown. In *Once Upon A Time In The West*, Cheyenne, suffering from a stomach wound, tells Harmonica that he hopes that whoever gets him knows how to shoot.

Time Code: 01:42:31
Information: Dialogue, "Before this tale of bloody revenge reaches its climax."

Time Code: 01:42:57
Information: Dialogue, between Bill and The Bride.

This lengthy dialogue scene between The Bride and Bill is inspired by the great apartment bound conversations between the male and female main characters of Godard's early films, especially

Breathless (1960), *Contempt* (1963), and *Band Of Outsiders*. The scene is also an extended reference to Ted Mikeis's *The Doll Squad* (1973), and its climactic conversation between Francine York and Michael Ansara, former lovers who are now opponents.

> **Time Code**: 01:43:49
> **Information**: Dialogue, "I call it 'The Undisputed Truth.'"

The Undisputed Truth is also a Motown band from the early '70s. In the original screenplay, Bill was also something of an alchemist, brewing various behavior controlling potions.

> **Time Code**: 01:44:13
> **Information**: Dialogue, Bill's Superman story.

The biggest cultural reference in the film is this one to Superman. It's not found in the online script. The essence of Bill's speech is that — unique to Superman — *Clark Kent* is the alias, unlike, say, Spider-Man, who's really Peter Parker, or Batman, who's really Bruce Wayne. Kent represents Superman's view of human beings, i.e., that we're all "weak, unsure, cowardly."

This whole idea comes from the foreword to Jules Feiffer's book THE GREAT COMIC BOOK HEROES. Feiffer writes on pages 18-19: "The particular brilliance of Superman lay not only in the fact that he was the first of the super-heroes, but in the concept of his alter ego. What made Superman different from the legion of imitators to follow was not that when he took off his clothes he could beat up everybody — they all did that. What made Superman extraordinary was his point of origin. Clark Kent. Remember, Kent was not Superman's true identity as Bruce Wayne was the Batman's or (on radio) Lamont Cranston the Shadow's. Just the opposite. Clark Kent was the fiction ... Superman only had to wake up in the morning to be Superman. In his case, Clark Kent was the put-on ... Kent existed not for the purposes of the story but for the reader. He is Superman's opinion of the rest of us, a pointed caricature of what we, the non-criminal element, were really like."

There is also a Superman story in the romantic comedy *Addicted to Love* (1997), starring Meg Ryan, which Tchéky Karyo, as a transplanted French restaurateur, tells to Matthew Broderick, by way of explaining his exoticness to Americans.

Time Code: 01:46:22
Information: Dialogue, "A-so."

Bill repeats his catch phrase from the chapel.

Time Code: 01:46:54
Information: Dialogue, "A natural born killer."

From Tarantino's film, but also a common phrase.

Time Code: 01:47:04
Information: Dialogue, "Working in a used record store..."

The work theme is revisited. The Bride is about to explain why she "switched jobs," so to speak.

Time Code: 01:50:56
Information: Image, Karen Kim's garb.

Some internet posters have suggest that Karen Kim's hotelier's costume was inspired by the look of the villainess in Sonny Chiba's first *Streetfighter*. A quick viewing of the film failed to substantiate this thoroughly.

The Bride's remark during the stand off that she is the "deadliest women in the world" harks back to *Pulp Fiction*'s *Fox Force Five* pilot description of her as the "deadliest women in the world with a knife."

The way that The Bride holds her gun on Karen Kim is reminiscent of the way Anne Parillaud does it in *La Femme Nikita* (1990), and its American remake, *Point Of No Return* (1993), with Bridget Fonda.

Time Code: 01:53:59
Information: Dialogue, "Before that strip turned blue I would have jumped a motorcycle onto a speeding train."

Maggie Cheung does this very thing in the Jackie Chan film *Chao ji ji hua* (1993) also known as *Supercop* or *Police Story 3*. There's also a similar scene in the more recent *Torque*.

Time Code: 01:54:13
Information: Dialogue, "Not anymore."

Motherhood has turned The Bride away from killing. She also doesn't want Bill to claim her (the way Esteban claims the children of his whores?). One could argue that this change in The Bride is under-motivated, since we don't see much of her before the change of heart, but her reaction to most youngsters throughout the movie is sympathetic and indulgent.

Time Code: 01:54:55
Information: Dialogue, "She would have been born into a world she shouldn't have."

The source, perhaps, for The Bride's rage as she hugs B.B. and looks at Bill when she first arrives.

Time Code: 01:56:18
Information: Dialogue, "In the third month of mourning you…"

Timeline information. The Bride was on the loose for three months before Bill accidentally stumbled upon her.

Time Code: 01:56:49
Information: Dialogue, "I overreacted."

Imagine Warren Beatty saying that line.

Time Code: 01:58:10
Information: Dialogue, "You and I have unfinished business."

The third time The Bride says this in the movie, and with the same lethal results.

Time Code: 01:58:31 – 01:58:42
Information: Music cue, "Invisible Pole Fighter" reprise.

As The Bride kills Bill.

Time Code: 01:58:46
Information: Music cue, "The Demise of Barbara" reprise.

More by Morricone.

Time Code: 01:59:12
Information: Dialogue, "I don't know. Because I'm a bad

person."

Why didn't The Bride say that Pai Mei had taught her his deadly technique? A part of her needed to withhold a trump card from Bill, despite their union.

Time Code: 01:59:39
Information: Dialogue, "Every once in a while you can be a real cunt."

Cunt is to *Kill Bill* what the word "nigger" is to *Jackie Brown* and "fuck" is to *Pulp Fiction*.

Time Code: 02:02:07
Information: Image and dialogue, Heckle and Jeckle cartoon.

The Talking Magpies, a Fox Terrytoon from 1946. At 02:02:23, Do you have a magpie in your home? The magpie is the most charming bird in the world." Is Tarantino here commenting through film on his reputation as a magpie artist, ripping off everything he sees?

Time Code: 02:02:16
Information: Image, BB in a motel room.

Motel rooms appear in almost all of Tarantino's films, and this moment is a lot like *Pulp Fiction*'s.

Time Code: 02:02:33
Information: Image, Lucky Charms cereal.

Matches Kaboom see way back at the start of the film.

Time Code: 02:02:40
Information: Image, The Bride from overhead on the floor of the bathroom weeping.

The last image of The Bride prone. Tears turn to laughter.

Time Code: 02:03:17
Information: Dialogue, "Thank you."

Who is The Bride thanking? Based on her little attended to "God's will" speech early in *Vol. 1*, I would guess God. The obliqueness of this moment has been likened by some posters to the mysterious shot of an implacable Greta Garbo that ends *Queen Christina* (1933).

Time Code: 02:03:27
Information: Music cue, "Malaguena Salerosa."

By Rodriguez's band, Chingon.

Time Code: 02:03:52
Information: Title card, "The lioness has rejoined her cub and all is right in the jungle."

The film ends in the spirit of another great female-killer-and-child film, *The Long Kiss Goodnight* (1996), directed by Renny Harlin, and starring Gena Davis and Samuel L. Jackson.

Time Code: 02:06:35
Information: Title card, "A.K.A., Snake Charmer."

Finally we learn Bill's codename.
This rehash of the cast comes from Ford films such as *The Quiet Man*.

Time Code: 02:06:53
Information: Title card, "AKA Mommy."

The last sobriquet for The Bride.

Time Code: 02:07:17
Information: Music cue, "Goodnight Moon."

By the cult group, Shivaree, with the appropriate lyric, "There's a blade by the bed / And a phone in my hand."

Time Code: 02:07:36
Information: Title card, "Uma Thurman."

The titles begin all over again.

Time Code: 02:08:09
Information: Title card, the question mark over Daryl Hannah.

This moment has filled fans with the hope for a sequel.

Time Code: 02:09:01
Information: Title card, "Martial Arts Adviser, Yuen Wo Ping."

Time Code: 2:09:58
Information: Image, The Bride winks.

Time Code: 02:09:17
Information: Title card, "Robert Richardson."

This credit offers the perfect opportunity to explore the complex relationship between Quentin Tarantino and Oliver Stone, especially as it betrays itself in *Kill Bill Vol. 1.*

As everyone knows, Oliver Stone adapted one of Tarantino's early screenplays, which came to the screen as his version of *Natural Born Killers*. There is a long and complicated genesis behind that adaptation, recounted one-sidedly in the book by *Killer Instinct*, co-producer and former Tarantino friend Jane Hamsher's account of the film's making. It is known that Tarantino wasn't particularly happy with the way the film came out, and supposedly doesn't really like to talk about it. On page 77 of *Quentin Tarantino: Interviews*, from the University of Mississippi Press, reprinting a chat with Joshua Mooney for *Movieline*, Tarantino says the most he has ever said publicly about the situation, and possibly all he ever will say. Though he seems angrier with the producers than at Stone, he does reserve some ire for the man who reportedly "totally" rewrote the script, as some journalists put it (I'd like to hunker down with a comparison some day).

This controversy belies the influence that Stone has had on Tarantino.

Let's look at the evidence, which may amount only to a series of coincidences. Both men are screenwriters and directors. Both court controversy, whether consciously or not, whether through language (the use of the word "nigger"), violence, or politics. Both have won Oscars for screenwriting. Both have made movies in which DJs figure importantly (*Talk Radio* versus *Reservoir Dogs*).

But the analogies go a little deeper than that.

Both are obsessed cinematically with violence, cars, and the American landscape be it rural areas, roads, the desert, or the Valley. Both have a complex relationship with Asian culture, which is more oblique in Stone and born of his Vietnam experience, if nothing else. The interest in cars and violence is shared by most American filmmakers and their movies but there is little doubt that both Tarantino and Stone have brought something peculiarly their own to the subjects.

Now, in *Kill Bill*, Tarantino uses Stone's best cinematographer, Robert Richardson. He also casts another Stone vet in an important part, Daryl Hannah, who was the temptress in *Wall Street*. He includes a cartoon anime sequence, which is akin to the sit-com sequence in *NBK* (or did Tarantino write that, too?).

Kill Bill is all about vengeance, and vengeance is a hidden theme in Stone's films: *Nixon*, *JFK*, *Platoon*, and *Wall Street* all hinge on acts of complexly motivated vengeance. In *Kill Bill*, the inspiration for the vengeance is pretty clear-cut, but is still the engine that drives the movie.

It's easy to see how the strange symbiotic relationship between Stone and Tarantino could go unnoticed. First there is the public animosity. Then there is the fact that Stone's films don't seem to mirror anything in Tarantino's films (unless the black population of *Any Given Sunday* is a shout out). Part of the problem is that Stone is not exactly as quotable as some of the B directors Tarantino worships. In fact, Stone is something of a square. He's the guy who managed to make a rock and roll movie (*The Doors*) squarer than even *Almost Famous*. Stone just doesn't seem as movie mad as Tarantino. Stone doesn't really talk that much about movies per se in his interviews. He talks about ideas. Controversies. Intentions. For Tarantino to acknowledge Stone in his films with subtle citations is tantamount to Nicholas Ray or Samuel Fuller in the '50s paying quaint visual homage to Stanley Kramer.

So what are we to make of this connection between

Tarantino and Stone? Like many of us, Tarantino probably has a love-hate relationship with Stone, but *unlike* the rest of us, he has actually tangible reasons for the hate part. In his view, Stone messed with his work. It's true that Tarantino is much more influenced by a couple of thousand B movie directors, and among A-list helmers Tony Scott looms larger. Plus, Stone's particular obsessions – deserts and Indians – hold no allure for Tarantino. Yet he cannot help but be influenced by Stone, because Oliver Stone is a vivid director, and because Stone's own career can serve as a model to a young man attempting to make his own mark on the industry.

Time Code: 2:10:02
Information: Music cue, the theme song from *Lady Snowblood*.

A reprise from the previous Volume.

Time Code: 02:11:119
Information: Title card, Editorial Production Assistants, Jasmine Yuen-Carrucan."

See earlier discussion of Jasmine's name.

Time Code: 02:13:31
Information: Music cue, "Black Mamba," the RZA.

Time Code: 02:15:44
Information: Title card, "Special Thanks, Robert Rodriguez, 'My Brother.'"

The two met at the Toronto Film Festival when Tarantino was promoting *Reservoir Dogs*. Later they both ended up at Miramax and contributed to *Four Rooms*. Rodriguez directed Tarantino's *From Dusk Till Dawn*, in which the writer also starred. Rodriquez did some of the music for *Vol. 2*, and Tarantino has returned the favor by directing a scene in Rodriquez's *Sin City*. They are less brothers, one would guess, than "friends" in the Hollywood sense, warriors of equal strength who circle each other warily but have decided not to kill each other.

Time Code: 02:15:44
Information: Title card, "Moon Sun Kwak."

Unknown.

Time Code: 2:15:44
Information: Title card, "Katsu Hito Ishii."

The writer and director of the films *The Taste of Tea* (2004) and *Party 7* (2000).

Time Code: 2:15:48
Information: Title card, "Sogo Ishii."

Japanese director of *Yume no ginga* (*Labyrinth of Dreams* 1997). Did this director's name end up lent to O-Ren?

Time Code: 2:15:48
Information: Title card, "Bento Fukasaku."

The son of Kenji Fukasaku, and a director in his own right.

Time Code: 2:15:48
Information: Title card, "Guillermo Navarro."

Tarantino's cinematographer on *Jackie Brown*, but most associated with Robert Rodriguez.

Time Code: 2:15:48
Information: Title card, "Mauricia Grant."

Unknown.

Time Code: 2:15:48
Information: Title card, "Peter Bogdanovich."

A fellow director who has loomed with special importance in recent years. They have a lot in common. Both love the books of Larry McMurtry. Both toiled on interview books on directors (Tarantino's was never finished). Both have had careers with dramatic rises and falls.

Time Code: 2:15:48
Information: Title card, "Stacy Sher."

A long-time associate of Tarantino's, whom he met when Jersey Films sponsored the early development of *Pulp Fiction*. Her name is also found as Stacey Sher.

Time Code: 2:15:48
Information: Title card, "Ada Shen."

Unknown.

Time Code: 2:15:48
Information: Title card, "Sarah L. Driver."

The namesake of Elle Driver, she is under her other/real name, Sarah Kelly, also the director of *Full Tilt Boogie*, a documentary about the making of *From Dusk Till Dawn*.

Time Code: 2:15:48
Information: Title card, "Sofia Coppola."

The woman Tarantino was dating at the time, Sofia Coppola is Hollywood royalty, the daughter of Francis Ford Coppola, and an Oscar winner in her own right, for *Lost In Translation*. Both Coppola (*The Godfather Part III*) and Tarantino are derided by harsh critics for being bad actors.

Time Code: 2:15:48
Information: Title card, "Eli Roth."

A new enthusiasm of Tarantino's. Roth directed the excellent *Cabin Fever* (2002), and had a bit part in *Terror Firmer*, which qualified him to do a full-length audio commentary of the film for the DVD release.

Time Code: 2:15:48
Information: Title card, "Rick Linklater."

Richard Linklater, the Austin-based director of *Slackers*, *Before Sunrise*, and *Waking Life*.

> **Time Code**: 2:15:49
> **Information:** Title card, "Jerry Martinez."

An old friend of Tarantino's from the Video Archives days. He has contributed to most of Tarantino's movies.

> **Time Code**: 2:15:48
> **Information:** Title card, "Mike Simpson."

Tarantino's agent at William Morris.

> **Time Code**: 2:15:59
> **Information:** Title card, "Kurt Russell."

The actor most associated with Tarantino-favorite John Carpenter gets special thanks.

> **Time Code**: 2:16:01
> **Information:** Title card, "The Gang at Ruby's."

Presumably the chain of 1940s style diners, created by Doug Cavanaugh and Ralph Kosmides in the early '80s. There are 22 in the Los Angeles area.

> **Time Code**: 2:16:01
> **Information:** Title card, "Burt Reynolds."

The actor-director allowed use of music from White Lightning.

> **Time Code**: 2:16:01
> **Information:** Title card, "Ap-Ron."

Unknown.

> **Time Code**: 2:16:08
> **Information:** Title card, "Eddie Brant's Saturday Matinee –

Los Angeles, Kim's Video and Music – New York, 42 Chamber of Shaolin – New York."

Favored video stores. Eddie Brant's is at 5006 Vineland Avenue in North Hollywood; one location for Kim's is 2906 Broadway in Manhattan.

Time Code: 2:15:48
Information: Title card, "And RIP Charles Bronson, Cheng Cheh, Sergio Corbucci, Lucio Fulci, Lo Lieh, Sergio Leone, Lee Van Cleef, William Witney."

Repeated from *Vol. 1*, with some additions. Spaghetti western directors Sergio Corbucci and Sergio Leone, and star Lee Van Cleef, are added, along with horror director Lucio Fulci, all to reflect the "spaghetti" concerns of the second film; Fukasaku and Shintaro "Zatoichi" Katsu are dropped.

Time Code: 2:16:36
Information: Coda, an outtake of Thurman as The Bride doing the eye plucking gag from the House of Blue Leaves.

A reward for those who stay through the credits. Thurman's enthusiasm for the job is infectious.

TWO

A BRIEF "KILL BILL" VOL. 2 ANTHOLOGY

Introduction

A really good anthology of *Kill Bill* reviews could easily be compiled, something along the lines of the mass market on *2001* that gathered together virtually everything published on that movie within a two year time frame. This is not that book. What follows is a small sampling of reviews of *Kill Bill Vol. 2*, and some meditations on *Kill Bill* as a whole. Time and budgetary constraints restricted me to familiar writers and to especially outstanding essays. What follows is just a hint of the diversity of opinion from movie reviewers in the mainstream media and found in Internet chat sites. The forthcoming academic response should be just as interesting.

Kill Bill Vol. 2
by Kim Morgan

The Bride is back and not soon enough for fans of Quentin Tarantino's *Kill Bill Vol. 1*, a bloody brilliant pastiche of grindhouse chop-sockey, samurai and Yakuza pictures, spaghetti Westerns, '70s chick flicks, blaxploitation films — and then some — wrapped up in that gorgeously violent package of an iconic Uma Thurman. Marlene, Bette, Rita, Clint, and now Uma — in her simultaneously modern and classic visage, she is the most forceful and seriously feminine female movie star currently on screen.

So enter our blonde goddess, a.k.a. Black Mamba, as she continues her "roaring rampage" to rub out those who left her for dead before her very low-rent and very pregnant El Paso wedding four years prior. Not one to change her priorities from the last time we saw her, she exclaims in the film's opening segment (shot 1940s film-noir-style complete with rear screen projection) that she is "gonna kill Bill." And *Kill Bill Vol. 2*, or rather, the next chapter, begins.

For those who need a refresher, The Bride has so far traveled from Tokyo and not only slaughtered an army of Yakuza, but more importantly, one of the DiVAS (Deadly Viper Assassination Squad) who did her wrong, O-Ren Ishii (Lucy Liu). She's also killed ex-DiVAS Vernita Green (Vivica A. Fox) in her modest house in Pasadena, California, and luckily, missed quick death at the hands of Elle Driver (perfect DiVA and wickedly sexy Daryl Hannah) in an inspired Brian De Palma-esque hospital sequence. Completing The Bride's (literal) eye-popping carnage in "The House Of Blue Leaves," the unseen Bill (David Carradine) asks, "Is she aware her daughter is still alive?"

Well, no, but in *Kill Bill 2*, there's a stronger sense of mission given to The Bride that suggests she may have something gnawing in her gut past simple vengeance. It's not that she's pissed, it's that she's got an instinct beyond her perfected killer chi. Fleshed out and humanized, The Bride (finally we're given her name — Beatrix Kiddo) is allowed to be vulnerable, heartbroken, even happy. She's a lovely character and a unique one — how often do you fall for the lady who plucks out another's eye?

Talkier and slower than *KB1*, *KB2* allows Beatrix more backstory, showing viewers the extended version of what transpired during her ill-fated wedding. Bill shows up (she hears his flute outside the chapel) and The Bride is unsteady and unprepared for what will happen next. You can see immediately that Beatrix and Bill were lovers and, as evil as he may seem, their two broken hearts are apparent. Beatrix chose to run away and start a new life while Bill couldn't allow the escape. In his assassin, kung-fu way, Bill is a pimp, and his prize possession (or one he loves best) is not leaving the brothel.

We then see how much Bill respected his young protégé when witnessing her tutelage under the severe instruction of Pai Mei (Chinese martial-arts star Gordon Liu), a white bearded monk who teaches her how to punch through wood and exact a five-point exploding-heart trick. Shot in '70s chop-sockey style with quick close-ups and jarring punctuations of fierceness, this sequence is not only an homage to Tarantino's beloved Shaw Brothers studios, it explains some of the techniques Beatrix uses later in the film.

Moving on to Mexico, we come across Budd (former DiVA Michael Madsen), Bill's poignantly drawn kid brother. Now something of a wash-up, working at a strip joint and living in a trailer, he's warned of The Bride's coming (or second coming) and, though understanding of her rage, sees no problem in making her suffer whilst attempting to kill her. Without giving too much away, we'll just say this: buried alive is something even Black Mamba can crack.

Meanwhile, Elle Driver slinks her way into Budd's place with a parcel of a million dollars in exchange for Beatrix's Hattori Hanzo sword. Speeding along in her black Trans Am in her black suit and eye-patch, Elle is all business. But the woman we initially thought of as possessing mere hatred shows a little respect to Black Mamba — how dare Budd knock her off in such an unsavory, disrespectful manner.

Of course Beatrix isn't rubbed out, which leads us to the film's conclusion — one that gives the picture even more substance and texture. Bill (played so splendidly by Carradine — you can't imagine anyone else in the role) is offered a terrific speech (about Superman), Beatrix is given an explanation ("I overreacted," Bill says, to which she replies incredulously, "You overreacted?"), and, importantly, some secrets are revealed.

But they won't be revealed here. As an extension of the first installment (this is *one* film after all), the picture becomes an epic work on many levels. It's a woman's picture, beyond the tired "girls kick ass" type. It's a love story between two very similar people at odds with a very normal, square world. It's an action picture that, in an inspired sequence, pits two very capable assassins against each other in a tiny trailer. It's brilliantly choreographed, beautifully filmed, wonderfully scored, and lovingly acted with an old fashioned, stylized, formal manner of speaking that drips out of characters' mouths casually. It's a genre-drenched geek-fest that wears its film-reference love so much on its sleeve that it moves well beyond movie name-dropping. *Kill Bill 2* becomes an entity all its own: recognizable, yet wholly refreshing, and by its final scene, touching. A lot of critics say this, and much too often, but truly, Quentin Tarantino has completed a film that exemplifies *why* we go to the movies. He loves movies; we love movies. And both director and viewer love the very fact that these pieces of celluloid can take on a life of their own. That kind of movie life is raised to such an extraordinary degree here that we leave the experience swooning.

Kill Bill Vol. 2
by David Walker

A hyperactive explosion of stylish violence and splattering guts, Quentin Tarantino's *Kill Bill Vol. 1* was a pastiche of cinematic references and grindhouse aesthetics. With Uma Thurman cutting a bloody swath through those who done her wrong, *Kill Bill* was more action than story, more style than substance. And as the first half of Tarantino's epic tale of retribution drew to a bloody, cliff-hanging climax, the promise of an equally visceral, brilliant conclusion hung in the balance. But now that *Kill Bill Vol. 2* has finally arrived, the eager anticipation is over and it's time for the … well … disappointment? Picking up where *Vol. 1* left off — it is all one big film, after all — *Vol. 2* does an about-face, trading all the breakneck energy of the first for exposition and dialogue. As a film in and of itself, *Kill Bill Vol. 2* isn't bad (although it is Tarantino's weakest movie). But as the second half of a larger story, it fails to complement its mate. And at times *Vol. 2* seems more like a work by one of the imitators Tarantino has spawned than something by the man himself.

Kill Bill Vol. 2
by Damon Houx

When we last left The Bride (Uma Thurman), she had just sliced her way through two members of her kill list, Go-Go Yubari, Johnny Mo, and the fifty-seven members of the Crazy 88 (as Bill tells us in this volume, "They just called themselves 'The Crazy 88'" because, as he guesses, "they thought it sounded cool.") And after the uproarious, immoral, and gonzo first section, the series (which was split into two because of its unwieldy running time) mutates into something else. Something extraordinary.

Both films are divided into five chapters, with the last chapters the longest, and the end of the first film is meant to be a cliffhanger — the last words spoken are "Is she (The Bride) aware her daughter is still alive?" This ending sets up the dramatic tonal shift of the second half. Implicit in it is that — in the hoariest of action clichés — with *Vol. 2*, this time it's personal. And it is; the first film had The Bride hacking through numerous people, but none whom she was that close to or cared about. Here the body count is reduced to focus on the people that The Bride must kill to enact her bloody revenge (there are only three on-screen deaths, and the reviewer would like to note that those who've seen the film and might doubt him should think of fish heads). And for these three names left on the kill list, it's a different but no less engaging ride.

After the violent introduction that accompanies both films and some brief remarks from The Bride, the story kicks off with a flashback to the "Massacre At Two Pines," where Bill (David Carradine) set the "whole gory story" in motion. Immediately, the change of tone is apparent, as — after an amusing introduction of how the wedding would go (with Bo Svenson as the priest and a cameo from one of Q.T.'s regulars) — Bill gets his first on-screen moments. Immediately, Bill and The Bride's relationship is deepened; though we know both what is about to happen and that it's Bill's baby, both characters have a certain longing and appreciation for each other. Sweeping out of the church to reveal the assassins on the prowl, the unavoidable tragedy gains a new sense of melancholy, something that has been evident in the first half, but is all the more present here.

Then we meet Budd (Michael Madsen), who refuses brother Bill's help, insisting on dealing with The Bride himself. Though introduced in *Vol. 1* as perhaps accepting of The Bride's revenge, he's revealed to be something of a shitkicker who sold his Hattori Hanzo sword for some dough. Working at a titty bar as the bouncer, we see that his life has become filled with desperation as he takes his personal licks from his coked-out boss (Larry Bishop, owning his scant screen time). But Budd is tougher than he looks and tricks The Bride, allowing him to have the chance to bury her alive.

The story then flashes to The Bride's training with kung-fu master Pai Mei (Gordon Liu, returning from *Vol. 1*, albeit as a totally different character). Pai Mei is a bastard, but he trains her in the ways she will use to escape, while also allowing Tarantino to pay his Shaw Brothers homage by replicating their techniques (odd zooms, beard stroking), their fu styles (Five Point Palm Exploding Heart Technique), and their cadence ("You are as helpless as a worm fighting an eagle.") It's worth noting that Pai Mei is based on a Shaw Brothers character of the same name who'd — as Tarantino notes in the supplements — often fight against Shaw regular Liu. Budd has promised The Bride's new sword to Elle Driver (Daryl Hannah), and they exchange unpleasantries until Elle gets what she wants. But she too must have her showdown against The Bride (whose name is revealed in such a way that it seems to have been kept secret in the first volume to make a joke of Bill's opening remarks to her). This all leads into the final chapter, where The Bride must face down Bill. But — as the audience knows — he has their daughter B.B. (button-cute Perla Haney-Jardine), and both parties have some unanswered questions before their final *mano a mano* can take place.

It would be easy to repeat what has been said about the first film and its high points: the sound design, Robert Richardson's excellent cinematography, Tarantino's (and original music providers The RZA's and Robert Rodriguez's) great ear for music, Yuen Wo Ping's brutal and brilliant fight choreography are still great here. But what makes this the better film of the two is its depth. One of the things that define great art is that it comes alive because of the minutia. Artists who know their subjects create believable worlds out of them — the best stories not only ask us to fill in the blanks, but make those blanks seem natural to fill. And where *Vol. 1* was all femme-centric hyperkinetic and hyperstylized violence, here we are faced with four characters who are deadly, but also well defined.

Though there is no denying the comeback power of David Carradine's performance, Michael Madsen delivers the film's best male turn. From the end of the first volume he is introduced being a bit more melancholy, but his performance and character have many interesting — and sometimes contradictory — layers. Budd tells Bill that he sold his Hanzo sword in El Paso for $250, but it is later revealed that he kept it. What we know from the first chapter (and first film) was that The Bride was assaulted in El Paso, making his sword sale metaphorical — he knows he crossed a line, and his life-change reflects this shame. How else can one interpret Budd's new life? At one time Budd was one of the toughest men alive (one assumes from his role in the Deadly Viper Assassination Squad), and yet he takes all the crap dished out at him by his boss — why else take it except some form of penance? With his razor-blade necklace and chew-spitting ways, he's both dumber and smarter than he looks, and one's aware of these complicated emotions inside him.

And never is this clearer than — in one of the great moments of the series — the odd look he gives The Bride when he's about to bury her. "This is for my brother," he says, yet he obviously has divorced himself from that side of his life. In another movie his actions might seem like bad writing, but here the character is obviously divided on his involvement in the whole process (as he drawls, "That woman deserves her revenge … and … we deserve to die … but then again, so does she … so, I guess … we'll … just see, won't we?") When Budd meets his fate, one almost feels a bit sorry for him. Almost.

And though we've learned of the wrath of Elle Driver in the first half, here we get to know her real character. Not only is she a real bitch, but her relationship to Bill (especially in light of Bill and The Bride's relationship) becomes all too clear: Elle has always been second best. Eager to please Bill, she's never been fond of The Bride because of her favored status, and has relished the last few years as the new number one. She's also obviously petulant, and acts like The Bride's lesser sibling. Her fate is far more relishable. And it is in these sections that Tarantino gets to play more homages than he does in the film's second Bill-centric half, as the Leone Westerns (heightened by the rampant use of Ennio Morricone's music) and the *giallo* in general (the burial, and a mutilation).

Which brings us and The Bride to Bill, and David Carradine. Made a mysterious and off-screen presence in the first film, he is introduced minutes into the second half, and becomes a dominating presence throughout. It's interesting to note that Warren Beatty was in talks to play the role, since the Bill character — nicknamed The Snake Charmer — is surrounded by a bevy of women (his stable of killers is all women, excepting his brother) who do his pleasure; had Beatty played him, the film might have seemed more a commentary on Beatty and the numerous women he's romanced in his life. With Carradine, the warmth and affection that Bill has for The Bride shines through more; Beatty might have been more politically interesting, but Carradine is at a better service to the character and becomes another one of Tarantino's great rediscovered actors; Carradine positively *shines* here.

The most interesting reveal about Bill is that he truly, madly, and deeply loves The Bride. Like her, he may be a "natural born killer," but he is shown to be affectionate and caring with their daughter, and the greatest reveal in this volume is how much the massacre in Two Pines was done (as Bill states at the beginning of both films) as an act of masochism. The viewer also is struck that Bill is not a bad father. Perhaps he too felt the redemptive effects of parenthood. One knows that the squad dissolved after the massacre

— a signal that that event changed everyone's life involved — while Bill muses to his daughter that "I knew what would happen to mommy if I shot her, what I didn't know was when I shot mommy what would happen to me." The last act, the near-hourlong final chapter, reveals that Bill was raised fatherless and (undoubtedly) has abandonment issues; though his violence was not reasonable, it was certainly justifiable to him.

And as the reason for his revenge on her is revealed so are her reasons for facing his wrath. What becomes apparent in this section is that the whole four-hour-plus journey is about two people who love each other, but have done such things to hurt the other, and that hurt so deep that they have no choice but to try and kill each other. It's an oddly poetic journey, metaphorical of many passionate but ultimately destructive relationships, though one that flaunts its amoral nature (all the main players, outside of B.B., are murderers.) In the end, the film becomes a perverted love story; a cumulative moment in Tarantino's oeuvre, since he has dealt with murderous lovers in two screenplays (that, coincidentally again, also started out as one film) in *True Romance* and *Natural Born Killers*. Here though, these two predators can no longer stay together once a child enters their lives.

Introducing a child into this world of violence is fitting, though transgressive to many viewers. The first volume's most awkward moment has The Bride facing the daughter of someone she murdered, and it's a moment that struck many critics as the film's greatest fault; ironically the moment that the "fun" violence becomes all too real (which, again, points out that many critics don't think through their reactions; aren't they saying that Tarantino's simply made the violence affecting?) But Tarantino is conscious of the effect both real and fake violence has, and the scars it leaves. Like Sam Fuller in *Naked Kiss*, Tarantino is optimistic that bad people can change, and when Bill and The Bride have their epic conversation before their showdown, in which Bill uses a truth serum to make sure his lover will be honest, it's revealed The Bride's escape from her life as a high-paid contract killer was done to preserve the integrity of her child's life and innocence. The sticking point for many is that B.B. enjoys watching *Shogun Assassin*, but later on B.B. is shown watching a cartoon that is equally violent; this may be the first political message Tarantino has ever crafted, in that he seems to be commenting on how others can unfairly judge what's acceptable for children without actually watching what's considered "good" children's entertainment. Ultimately there is a big difference between violence that's fake and violence that's real.

As entertaining as the series is, it wouldn't work if it weren't for Uma Thurman. What becomes most apparent about her in this volume is how everyone she meets falls in love with her (director included). In the Pai Mei segments, one can sense that even this old man who hates American women develops affection for her during their first fight. She's a charmer. Even Bill's surrogate father, Esteban (Michael Parks, who like Liu returns in a different role), is immediately won over her by her, while (spoiler though this may be) in their last moments together Bill expresses that she is a great person, one of the best people in his life. Which he says after she's effectively *killed* him.

This love-fest may be why rumors have swirled about Quentin Tarantino and Uma Thurman's relationship with each other. This pair of movies, as trying as they might have been on everyone involved to make, are essentially a love-letter (perhaps a platonic love, perhaps unrequited or requited, it's not really fair to say) to the talents and charm of Ms. Thurman. These films, like the men in The Bride's life, swoon over her. As an audience member, it's hard not too as well. When the story wraps with a surprisingly upbeat conclusion, it's impossible to not wish The Bride the best of luck.

For those looking to watch the entirety of *Kill Bill*, the division is effective. The first half offers aesthetic pleasure, while *Vol. 2* is the ethical, character-driven piece. The fun of the first picture is in the gory, pumped-up mayhem, and whatever might have followed would have seemed anti-climatic if seen in total. Some viewers were disappointed by the second installment because it was unable to outdo the "House Of Blue Leaves" sequence. That said, how could it? Wouldn't The Bride killing a hundred people or more become repetitive? Knowing the story in whole, the conclusion has to be about Bill and The Bride, and there's no way to justify such an overblown battle at that part of the story. Tarantino wanted to include an over-the-top slaughter to show The Bride's prowess, but telling it later in the tale might make the conclusion anti-climatic, simply because it's hard to separate the pleasure of spectacle from the pleasure of well-rounded characters; there's room for both, but in the division both become better formed. As such, it's hard not to view these films as separate — though continuous — entities. That said, there is talk of releasing the whole thing put together in a deluxe-o DVD set, rumored as of this writing but not confirmed. How much is fanboy speculation and how much is reality has yet to be proven, although a cut-together version played at Cannes in 2004, while the online screenplay hinted at sequences that may or may not have been shot (only one deleted scene is included with this DVD release).

With this, we're led to Quentin Tarantino. Though many forecasted doom for this project (and many have been hankering for the boy wonder to fall flat on his face), both films grossed around $70 million domestically (the total budget is reported to be around $70 million, so by splitting the film in half it seems Miramax doubled the gross), while DVD sales on the first title were strong, and (as to be expected) the films were well received in overseas markets. Tarantino is still his own animal, still gets to call his own shots at Miramax, and still is one of the most revered and imitated directors working today. And this reviewer couldn't be happier about that.

But what does this bode for the future of Tarantino? Having taken six years off between *Brown* and these films, one felt the absence in the interim, and now we're no longer able to expect anything for a while. Who knows how long the next project will take? Or if he'll ever get around to finishing the script for *Inglorious Bastards*? While Q.T.'s already stated that he wouldn't mind doing a future chapter in the *Bill* saga by following Nikki, the daughter of slain DiVAS member Vernita Green, he's waiting until the young actress who played her gets a bit older. Like, fifteen to twenty years older.

What is apparent though, is that through these two efforts Tarantino made the movie-mad film people have been expecting since *Pulp Fiction*, the film that incorporated all the genres and filmmakers he loved into a magpie mélange. And yet, shockingly, *Kill Bill* is not only greater than the sum of its parts, but is also an emotionally effecting genre piece that (especially in this last chapter) nails not just the action but the characters and their burdens, making it a strangely affecting love story about "murdering bastards."

Miramax presents *Kill Bill: Vol. 2* in anamorphic widescreen (2.35:1), and both Dolby Digital 5.1 and DTS audio. And — like the first installment — it's a perfectly acceptable demo disc.

One hopes the gigantor box set does come someday, because there's little of worth here in terms of supplements. There's "The Making of *Kill Bill Vol. 2*" (26:03), which is a fairly good little featurette in comparison to most, but still slight. Chingon Performance from the *Kill Bill Vol. 2* Premiere (11:32) features co-composer Roberto Rodriguez performing music from the film, and is exactly that. What will whet many fans' appetites is the Damoe deleted scene (3:37), which features Michael Jai White and his gang squaring off against David Carradine because he killed White's master. It's a nice chance to watch the former *Kung Fu* star kick ass, with White's Australian accent, stilted laughs and "You bastard" dialogue meant to replicate the experience of bad dubbing. And shockingly, no trailers, even though there are a couple new ones that didn't make the first disc.

"You bastards" indeed.

- Color (with black-and-white sequences)
- Anamorphic widescreen (2.35:1)
- Single-sided, dual-layered disc (SS-DL)
- Deleted scene
- Featurette: "The Making of *Kill Bill Vol. 2*"
- Featurette: "Chingon Performance from the *Kill Bill Vol. 2* Premiere"
- Keep-case

Mother, Killer, Warrior, Bride:
Honor, Power, And Femininity in *Kill Bill*
by Jessica Harbour

"Don't get me wrong: you would have made a wonderful mother. But you are a killer."
— Bill (David Carradine) to Beatrix (Uma Thurman) in *Kill Bill Vol. 2*

In *Kill Bill* Tarantino creates a universe with its own, surprising particular set of rules. Mark Conard, writing for Metaphilm, a film criticism website, posited that the character of Beatrix makes the journey from femininity to masculinity and back again: she begins as a helpless receptacle (even the sheriff who discovers her dying in the wedding chapel describes her as a "tall drink of cocksucker"), takes up a Hattori Honzo sword in revenge, and finally rediscovers herself as a woman. As he describes the final fight between Beatrix and Bill:

Beatrix's sword is quickly flung away in the fight, and as Bill jabs his sword towards her, she sheathes it in the case she's still holding. If the sword has all along symbolized the penis and the power it represents, then the sheath is symbolically the vagina, now itself a symbol of power — and consequently the pussy overcomes the cock in this fight, the woman, *as woman and mother*, defeats the man, the father. Mommy kills daddy.

But I would say there's even more to it than that. The layers of *Kill Bill* come not only from its combination of the revenge drama and the mother-daughter bond — not all that frequently seen since the myth of Demeter searching for her lost daughter Persephone — but on its concepts of honor running around gendered lines. The women of *Kill Bill* run the gamut, from the concentratedly murderous Go-Go Yubari to the old biddy Mrs. Harmony, but the men can, essentially, be divided into two categories: those who respect Beatrix as a warrior and those who see her solely as a woman, or (as Conard notes) a pussy. The theme of the mother's revenge and the theme of sexual humiliation go hand in hand with a third theme — that of the strength that lies in bonds between women, unhindered by men. In *Kill Bill*, ultimately, power is a girl thing.

"Trix Are For Kids": O-Ren And Beatrix

The first thing to note about the two volumes of *Kill Bill* is their parallel structure. Each begins with a flashback to Bill's shooting Beatrix, the climax of the wedding chapel massacre. In both Beatrix is laid low — in *Vol. 1*, she's trying to regain her strength after four years in a coma; in *Vol. 2*, Budd has buried her alive — when she flashes back to a story of growing up and training: the coming-of-age story of O-Ren Ishii (Lucy Liu) in *Vol. 1*, Beatrix's own training with Pai Mei in *Vol. 2*. In both cases Beatrix emerges after the story re-energized, able to take on the "big" villain: O-Ren and her minions, including her knee-sock-clad "personal bodyguard" Go-Go Yubari, in *Vol. 1*, Bill himself in *Vol. 2*.

O-Ren's backstory is animated: a local Yakuza's thugs kill her parents on their bed while she's hidden underneath it; later she sneaks into the boss's bedroom, disguised as a child prostitute, and kills him. The second murder is explicitly sexual, the first drenched in sexual imagery: the killer's sword goes through the bodies of O-Ren's parents to where she's hiding beneath, and blood drips onto her face. To say O-Ren tortures and kills the man who robs her of her innocence is a euphemism but not a stretch. Then O-Ren, at her first dinner as chief Yakuza, decapitates a rival who mutters racist remarks about her parents. Of the four other DiVAS, it seems, O-Ren is the most likely to understand Beatrix's need for revenge.

Vol. 1 suggests that, among the DiVAS, O-Ren was the closest thing to a friend Beatrix had. Budd blames Beatrix for his brother's broken heart; she and Elle Driver hate each other, and her familiar banter with Vernita is tinged with hostility and fear. But when O-Ren, facing Beatrix down, begins a line — "Silly rabbit" — Beatrix completes it: "Trix are for kids."[1] Even O-Ren's mocking Beatrix as a "Caucasian girl" who can't handle a sword might be more than just taunting. Beatrix is apparently an old hand with samurai swords, as she tells Pai Mei she is "more than proficient," and Hattori Honzo himself never questions her knowledge. An energetic fanfic writer could easily imagine O-Ren calling Beatrix "Caucasian girl" as they trained together. While both Budd and Elle talk about the kind of death Beatrix "deserves" without any intention of giving it to her, O-Ren promises her an honorable death: "You may not fight like a samurai, but at least you can die like one." Finally, Beatrix cries only after two deaths: Bill's — and O-Ren's.

If *Vol. 1* is the explicit homage to the samurai genre, then, O-Ren is its best representative. Unlike Vernita, O-Ren doesn't try to talk Beatrix out of her quest for revenge, but simply accepts it, and kneels before her during the fight. O-Ren is also the only other female assassin who is apparently able to bond with other women, with Go-Go constantly at her side. When O-Ren decapitates the disrespectful Yakuza, Go-Go smiles; when Go-Go dies, O-Ren briefly caresses the short sword she leaves behind. It's worth noting that the two women who have apparently become Bill's lover after Beatrix's coma, Sofie and Elle Driver, are both left horribly maimed — they've allied themselves with a man, not with another woman. But O-Ren dies honorably, in combat, having herself acknowledged that the snow-covered garden is a beautiful last sight.

"Do You Want To Penetrate Me?": Sexual Humiliation And Go-Go's Revenge

Unlike O-Ren, Go-Go Yubari seems to kill just for the hell of it. Is she simply "psychotic," to quote Conard? Possibly not. Conard doesn't mention *Battle Royale*, the last film directed by the great Japanese director Kinji Fukasaku. Tarantino's respect for *Battle Royale* is no secret: he introduced it at a Fukasaku retrospective in New York in

2000, and includes Fukasaku in the "In Memoriam" credits of *Vol. 1*. More importantly for our purposes, Tarantino took two actresses from *Battle Royale*: Ai Maeda, who voices the young O-Ren in *Vol. 1*'s animated sequence, and Chiaki Kuriyama, who plays Go-Go.

It's worth looking at Kuriyama's character, Chigusa, in *Battle Royale*, where a group of schoolkids, on an island, are forced to kill one another or die trying. Midway through the film, Chigusa is hit on by Niida, a boy who has a crush on her. She isn't interested. He begs her to deflower him, then threatens her. The scene escalates until Chigusa kills Niida by repeatedly stabbing him in the groin. (Next to Kou Shibasaki's Mitsuko, and possibly ahead of Aki Maeda's Naoko — both of whom get about twice as much screen time — Chigusa is the most memorable female character in *BR*.)[2]

Sure enough, Go-Go's first fight onscreen isn't with Beatrix — it's with a man who propositions her in a bar; she immediately stabs him and laughs. This sequence *is* a joke — a rather sick one (especially coming from Tarantino) on every Japanese-schoolgirl-fanservice-story ever told. Go-Go doesn't need that much time onscreen; she's potent and violent enough. She knows how sick men can be; that's why she takes such pleasure twisting knives in their guts. It's as if Go-Go is continuing what Chigusa started.

Admittedly, Tarantino is cheating slightly if he's using Chiaki Kuriyama as a reference to the *Battle Royale* near-rape-turned-murder scene. But Go-Go's apparent hostility towards men and sexuality repeats what I see as the second enduring theme of the movie: a horror of sexual violence and sexual humiliation. Chris Orr, the online film critic for *The New Republic*, disgustedly read *Kill Bill*'s sexual violence as a series of jokes; they're not jokes. It's not a joke when Beatrix, just awakened from her coma, learns that a hospital orderly has been offering her helpless body up for the taking, and Tarantino films the pimp and the leering john from her prone point of view. Nor is the O-Ren animated flashback sequence presented as a joke, though it's so over –the top it could be mistaken for one. Finally, in *Vol. 2*, when Beatrix sees the prostitute who has been permanently disfigured by Esteban Vihaio, it's no joke: she stiffens, and where before she was playfully flirting with Vihaio, she returns to her mission: "Where's Bill?"

Budd, meanwhile, is the only one of the five assassins to use sexual taunts against Beatrix. After he gets fired from his degrading strip club job, Budd comes home; Beatrix attacks him there, but he shoots her with two bullets full of rock salt "in the tits" (his words). He ties her up and takes her to an open grave, presenting her to his accomplice as "blond pussy," then threatens to Mace her when she struggles. Budd's attempted murder of Beatrix is cruel past the point of honor, which Elle acknowledges when she arrives at Budd's trailer to buy Beatrix's sword. And of all the people killed, Budd suffers the worst, dying from a poisonous snakebite while Elle taunts him. The snake Elle uses is a Black Mamba, Beatrix's codename; Beatrix, who earlier killed, painfully, the john and the orderly pimp, now symbolically kills Budd.

Yet Budd has real respect for Beatrix: "That woman deserves her revenge," he tells his brother Bill. He buries her with a flashlight; if Budd knows about Beatrix's training with Pai Mei, it is entirely possible he expects her to rise from her trap, giving Elle a nasty shock (and him a million dollars). Like Vernita, he seems to have left the high life of assassinations without regret. He's not Elle; dishonorable behavior doesn't come naturally to him. Degraded and humiliated himself, he chooses to re-enact his humiliation on Beatrix, and it costs him.

Budd's death is followed by Beatrix's fight with Elle (and the revelation that Budd had not, as he claimed, pawned the sword Bill gave him as a gift — again, dishonor doesn't come naturally to him, even when he tries). Elle does not pose her threat to Beatrix in sexual terms, as Budd did, but she violates the movie's codes of honor. She attempted to poison a comatose Beatrix in *Vol. 1*, and had to be talked out of it by her lover Bill: "We are better than that." She insulted and later killed Pai Mei — not just Beatrix's *sifu*, but Bill's and, presumably, her own. Elle is also complicit in Beatrix's dishonorable burying alive — although she proclaims, "That woman deserved better," it has been, at most, 12 hours since Beatrix was buried; if Elle felt that strongly about it she could easily dig Beatrix up; instead she calls Bill and gloats. More important than jealousy — Beatrix never mentions, or even seems to know, that Bill said to Elle, "I love you very much" — is the fact that Elle fights dirty, and when she finally goes up against Beatrix in one-on-one combat, Beatrix bests her.

The Showdown Of Arlene Plympton And Jeannie Bell

The movie's first fight would seem to contradict the emphasis on power lying with honorable women. Beatrix goes to Vernita Green's home in suburban Pasadena and fights and kills her there. In the midst of this, Vernita's daughter Nikki, about the same age as Beatrix's lost child, gets home from school; she is sent out, only to return to find that Beatrix has thrown a knife into her mother's chest. The girl stands silent. Beatrix apologizes, and tells her that if she wants to, when she grows up, she can find Beatrix and kill her.

Some online writers wondered if this sequence was just a riff on the idea that the black person always gets killed first. I think, actually, it sets up all the movie's themes. Orr wondered why Beatrix, herself a grieving mother, so quickly killed Vernita after learning she had a daughter; but Orr leaves out that the initial betrayal was not Beatrix's but Vernita's. The parallels between the life Beatrix (as "Arlene Plympton") would have lived in El Paso and the life Vernita (as "Jeannie Bell") tries to live in Pasadena are near-identical: both women want to put their pasts behind them and live as housewives, raising their daughters in peace. But Vernita tries to claim this privilege for herself, having already denied it to Beatrix: she asks Beatrix to spare her for Nikki's sake, having earlier refused to spare Beatrix for the sake of *her* child. If O-Ren is Beatrix's most respectful opponent (save Bill), Vernita is the most craven.

But Vernita's death, and her daughter's lack of reaction to it, sets up the possibility that Beatrix will be unable to enter the mother-daughter, female-female bond she misses so much. Throughout the film, motherhood and death are hard to separate: Beatrix gives birth while "dead," and believes until she enters Bill's hacienda that her daughter is dead. Now she not only kills the mother but also at a stroke turns the daughter into a killer — when she originally ran away so that her own daughter would not become a killer. If it is impossible to be killer and mother at the same time, then Vernita's death sets up the possibility that Beatrix can never be anything but a killer.

This possibility is reinforced by the weird behavior of B.B., Beatrix's and Bill's daughter. She's a parody of a well-behaved child, seeming not at all surprised to see the mother she's never seen walk through the door, and accepting without complaint that Daddy put Mommy to sleep for four years. In one long sequence, Bill, while tenderly cutting the crusts off a sandwich for B.B., tells the story of B.B.'s first "kill" — the pet goldfish she stepped on. B.B. looks on without a tear. The final scene, where she watches cartoons as Beatrix privately weeps over Bill's death, suggests she feels nothing upon the death of her father. Bill is a monstrous father, calmly able to fire at Beatrix after letting B.B. fall asleep in her arms, and everything except Beatrix's joy and love suggests he has left behind a monstrous daughter, disconnected from death.

Lioness And Cub: The Transformation Of Beatrix
Now comes the time to talk about Bill's role in Beatrix's life. With remarkable economy, Tarantino establishes the affection and wariness between Bill and Beatrix; Bill once told her stories, addressed her affectionately as "Kiddo" and introduced her to his mentor, Pai Mei; she, in turn, desperately wants him to think well of her as he lets her go. The scene in the wedding chapel where Beatrix kisses him twice on the mouth, full of longing, and his lips barely move is (in my opinion) the best for both David Carradine and Uma Thurman, and the best in how much it says about both characters. As Conard rightly points out, the godlike Bill of *Vol. 1* is humanized, and therefore made vulnerable, in *Vol. 2*.

But then Beatrix visits Esteban Vihaio, a "father figure" of Bill's. Like father figure, like son: Esteban is smooth, charming — and vicious towards women. As Bill is the snake charmer, so Esteban is the pimp; they gather women, but the women are not safe. More than any scene with Bill himself, the brief scene with Esteban reminds us that Bill is, for all his respect for Beatrix and affection for B.B., evil.

But can Beatrix really protect B.B. from her own role as killer? She admits under Bill's truth serum that she didn't expect her life in El Paso to work. Elle and Sofie are still alive, and Vernita's daughter, presumably, lies in wait.[3] But the movie's penultimate fight suggests that Beatrix might be able to draw power from female-female bonds — now, her bond with her daughter — after all. When Bill asks why she left him, Beatrix flashes back to when she found out, on assignment, that she was pregnant (a scene of Beatrix scrambling around in a hotel bathroom, a chick-flick moment in a Tarantino film) and was immediately set upon by Karen, a shotgun-toting representative of the woman she's been assigned to kill. Guns drawn, Beatrix pleads with Karen to read the positive test. Karen does: "Say I did believe you. What then?" "Go home," Beatrix says. Karen does, but not before saying, "Congratulations." This is the second confrontation with the Asian-descent representative of an Asian-American woman Beatrix wants to kill — the first being Go-Go and O-Ren (the target's name is Lisa Wong). But this time, instead of destruction, it ends in mutual agreement, two women recognizing the transformative power of motherhood.

Then Beatrix tells Bill: "Before that strip turned blue, I was a woman. I was *your* woman." It's an interesting turn of phrase, given that motherhood would, in theory, reinforce Beatrix's femininity, not negate it. But in *Kill Bill*, to be "Bill's woman" — as Elle and Sofie later become — is to be isolated from the power that comes from bonding with other women. In this way Beatrix's becoming a mother to her daughter (and note that she refers to "my daughter" at the wedding chapel, before B.B. is even born) initiates her into the power of the female-female bond. Beatrix's days may be numbered and her daughter permanently warped, but she has rescued herself and her daughter from Bill. The power in this movie comes from female-female combinations: O-Ren, Sofie, and Go-Go; Vernita and her daughter; Beatrix and her daughter; even, briefly, "Arlene" and her loving female friends in El Paso. Beatrix's four longest fights are with O-Ren, Go-Go, Vernita, and Elle; by contrast she makes relatively short work of Bill.[4]

Kill Bill ends with the assertion that "the lioness is reunited with her cub." I think the word "cub" here is deliberate; it echoes *Lone Wolf And Cub*, the *manga* series that puts samurai showdowns in the context of a roaming father and his young son. (*Lone Wolf And Cub*, in its turn, owes a debt to *Shogun Assassin*, the movie B.B. and Beatrix watch together.) The word "reunited," meanwhile, reinforces B.B.'s instant recognition of her mother. The movie's moral universe is, however temporarily, restored to order: her revenge duties done, Beatrix can be a mother first and a killer second.

For me this makes *Kill Bill* more than just a thrill ride made up of one in-joke after another. References — Paula Schultz this and Ultimate Truth that — are the building blocks Tarantino uses, because he loves them, but what makes *Kill Bill* fascinating is that the blocks add up to a greater story of the powers of murder and motherhood, and feminine power. First Beatrix kills; then she kills because her child died; finally she kills so that her child can live, and sobs, "Thank you," not just for her daughter but for the completion of her journey.

References

Conard, Mark T., "*Kill Bill Vol. 2:* Mommy Kills Daddy," April 26, 2004. <http://metaphilm.com/philm.php?id=310_0_2_0>

Tarantino, Quentin, *Kill Bill*.
<http://www.killbill2.net/script.html#5>

Orr, Chris, "Dud Again," *The New Republic* Online, August 10, 2004.
<http://www.tnr.com/doc.mhtml?i=hmovies&s=orr081004>

Notes
1. After this line in the original script, there's a note: "This is something they used to say back when they fought alongside each other as 'Vipers.'"
2. It's worth noting here that, according to fan sites, Tarantino wanted Kou Shibasaki to play Yuki Yubari, Go-Go's sister, who would attack Beatrix to avenge Go-Go — again reinforcing the idea of pairs of women reinforcing each other's power. In *Battle Royale*, Shibasaki's character, Mitsuko, also originally appears to be killing solely for power and enjoyment, but in the 2001 edition of the film, additional scenes were added to show that Mitsuko was sexually abused as a child — again suggesting the link between sexual abuse and violence. Shibasaki, whose career in Japan is thriving, apparently turned down the role, and Tarantino wrote Yuki out of the script, but some of Go-Go's lines, and the scene where she stabs the businessman, were originally Yuki's.
3. Tarantino told *Entertainment Weekly* in April 2004 that he is considering making *Kill Bill Vol. 3*, with Ambrosia Kelly reprising her role as Nikki, trained by Sofie Fatale to take on Beatrix. If he does, it will be interesting to see if Nikki's experiences under a female mentor differ from Beatrix's experiences under her male mentors. And Budd makes, admittedly, relatively short work of her. Conard suggests Beatrix doesn't understand the change of genre, from samurai drama to Western: her sword no longer works. It is also possible that she expects an "honorable" fight, not knowing the extent of Budd's humiliation since she last saw him.

Tarantino and the Vengeful Ghosts of Cinema
by Maximilian Le Cain

"When you have to shoot, shoot. Don't talk."
– Tuco (Eli Wallach) standing over the still warm corpse of an excessively verbose enemy in *The Good, The Bad and The Ugly* (Sergio Leone, 1966)

It's a real shame when (Uma Thurman) finally faces Bill (David

Carradine) for their showdown at the end of *Kill Bill Vol. 2* (Quentin Tarantino, 2004). For a start, it means the fun's nearly over – couldn't Tarantino have somehow spun a dozen episodes out of this saga? (Bet Feuillade could've!) But it's also a very bad scene, an anticlimax to what otherwise might well have been the best – that is, the richest, most intelligent, unique and exciting – film to have come out of the Hollywood mainstream since Scorsese's *Casino* (1995). But the reasons that this scene fails are very revealing, illustrating why the rest of the film works so well and why it is different enough from Tarantino's previous work to finally win over even an inveterate Tarantino-sceptic like me.

Let's skip back to the beginning of the exquisite first "volume." Tarantino kicks off with visiting vengeance on ex-assassin, now devoted mum Vernita Green (Vivica A. Fox) in her immaculate suburban house, an advertiser's archetype of stable, affluent *normality*. After the two smash the pristine home and each other up a bit, their battle is interrupted by the return of Vernita's young daughter from school. She is boggle-eyed at the spectacle of these two bloodied women suddenly assuming a patently fake air of ordinariness – mummy's old friend just dropped in for a visit. The incredulous poppet is packed off to watch telly and the antagonists, after a brief conversation, proceed with their violence. The Bride comes out victorious. The little girl catches standing over her dead mother and is given a lecture on her right to claim vengeance when she grows up. This scene is significant in several ways, and we will return to it. What needs to be emphasised now is the extent to which it wilfully, almost gleefully demolishes the image of stable, everyday familial normality. It does so with a smirking humour that is all but contemptuous. The message is clear: abandon here any residual attachments to real life, including its values and ethics.

Flash forward to the end of part two when discovers that her little daughter is still alive and living with Bill, her father and 's ex-boyfriend. In the reunion scene Tarantino comes close to doing something truly brilliant – creating a radical, dazzlingly perverse body of familial ethics, a mutant normality to replace the one he demolished in the destruction of Vernita and her home. In a jaw-dropping "facts of life" talk, dad explains how he came to put a bullet in mum's head. He does so in terms of an analogy with the little girl's recent killing of her pet goldfish and the ineffectual remorse she felt afterwards. They feed her a sandwich and tuck her up in bed. Can she watch a video with mum? Sure. How about a slice of Japanese mega-violence like *Shogun Assassin* (Kenji Misumi & Robert Houston, 1980), the story of a samurai and his infant child on a revenge quest? Dad has his doubts, but mum agrees. After all, it's a special occasion – she's been "dead" for the past four years! So mother and daughter bond watching savage swordplay films and the little girl seemingly accepts the grand melodrama of her parents' story as adult normality.

At the risk of impertinence, it must be said that it would have been wonderful had Tarantino ended the film just there, with Bill and back together again, a happy couple. There are several reasons for this. Firstly, Tarantino is famed for playing surprising tricks on his audience. A film called *Kill Bill* that ends with Bill alive, a revenge film where revenge is ultimately unnecessary… that would be a smart trick! Besides, Uma Thurman and David Carradine are such a beautiful pair that it would have been satisfying to see them end up together. They both positively drip cinema. When was the last time a Hollywood film treated us to close ups of a male face as fascinating as Carradine's, as anachronistically iconic, a face of the Western whose lines and creases reflect the desert landscape? That this film marks something of a comeback for him only adds to the potency of this aura: it is as if he spent the past twenty years wandering the same desert as John Wayne in *The Searchers* (John Ford, 1956) or Harry Dean Stanton in *Paris, Texas* (Wim Wenders, 1984). Except that when he finally returned to civilization he didn't set about reuniting a family that would ultimately exclude him. Instead he filmed with Tarantino and destroyed a family. The out-of-time authority of his appearance is backed up by the impressive control of his performance, all deadly gentleness and lived-in irony, with a voice almost disturbingly reminiscent of Jason Robards's world-weary rasp. Publicity material seems keen to promote Uma Thurman as something of an anachronism, too, a throwback to the elegantly glamorous stars of the '30s and '40s, an avatar of Carole Lombard or Marlene Dietrich. Looking at her magnificently expressive eyes or full, sensitive mouth one might concede that lineage. The severe, almost robotic slimness of her body, on the other hand, belies it, working against the requisite aethereality with a hard edge of almost mechanistic toughness. This combination works perfectly for *Kill Bill*'s killer heroine, a role which is obviously intended to elevate her to the status of an icon. Together Bill and form a couple whose only context and only home can be the history of cinema or, more specifically, the history of cinema according to Tarantino. Thus there is, on a mythological level, a certain natural justice in Bill trying to kill before she can marry an ordinary man, not to avenge the hurt of her running out on him so much as to prevent the union of a creature of pure cinema with a "mere mortal" which, Bill would have us believe, could only have ended catastrophically. For, as the circumstances of Vernita's death announce, ordinary values have no purchase in this extravagant universe.

In most instances, larger-than-life movie characters who exist beyond the rules and limitations of normality are loners, outside of society, constantly faced not just with death but with extinction. But Bill and have a child and through that child – brought up with a comic book wisdom beyond good and evil – Tarantino has the chance of bringing *Kill Bill*'s structure full circle by proposing an alternative to the shattered normality-image of Vernita's home. (The hyper-mundanity of this home was after all, simply a disguised haven for another lethal killer – Buñuel would doubtless have approved!) From the impossible lives of his epic characters he could potentially create a new domestic ideal, as the epic becomes the banal for a child raised with cartoonish battles as background to the everyday gestures that make up her life. This new ideal would not be a perversion or poisoning of normal family life but rather a completely new value structure with the ethos of action cinema at its centre. This is as opposed to the devastating invasion of home life suffered by the little girl orphans or by the young O-Ren Ishii (as an adult, Lucy Liu), the pathologising intervention of monstrous circumstances that so often define the fate of action movie characters. The Bride's child's comparatively cosy upbringing is pragmatically geared towards making her not necessarily an action movie character, but an inhabitant of the world of pulp cinema nevertheless. She is a child of cinema, and there is something of a film nut's wish-fulfillment fantasy in having parents able to relate to the extremes of violent cinema and, instead of censuring or interdicting them, allowing those extremes not only to coexist with the tenets of a loving household, but to be integral to them. That these parents should also be protagonists of this cinema awards the otherwise imaginary concerns of a film-fevered young mind an adult importance unobtainable in reality.

This original and interesting outcome is unfortunately only semi-realised. As soon as the little one goes to sleep and the big confrontation commences, either Tarantino's inspiration dries up or else, faced with the weighty task of satisfactorily concluding his saga, he just loses his nerve. Instead of pushing his ruthless action movie pseudo-morality through to the bitter end, he does a sudden U-turn and pleads in terms of a traditional reality-based morality which he has thus far systematically purged from the movie. His sudden mushiness is utterly illogical, as infuriating as Samuel L. Jackson's "redemption" at the end of *Pulp Fiction* (1994) and far more damaging because here the entire movie hangs on the scene's outcome. The problem with these sudden renunciations is that the invocation of the noble intentions of redemption or, in this case, the desire to provide a normal family situation for a child, are both meaningless and hypocritical because they are without basis in the universe Tarantino has created. He arbitrarily appeals to values that he assumes are so strongly present in the audience *a priori* that he doesn't have to bother working them into the ethical mechanics of his cinema. The form this appeal takes in *Kill Bill* is an excruciatingly awful flashback in which , having just discovered that she is pregnant, lets an assassin who tries to kill her remain alive. In accordance with the logic of the rest of the movie, one would assume that her reaction would have been to strike out even more ferociously at her assailant to protect her unborn child. For the better part of four hours the audience has been treated to an exhilarating celebration of movie violence – one weak flashback is far from sufficient to convince us suddenly that this image of violence is abhorrent. There might have been some justification for this transformation had Tarantino created an insurmountable dichotomy between the world of the assassins and parenthood, but Bill is depicted as an excellent father. Furthermore, the possibility of reconciliation is open to who decides to reject it. One might choose to read the fact that ends up destroying one of her daughter's parents, as well as her home, as rich in irony – after all, is this not exactly what Bill did to set the whole revenge quest in motion? But the fact remains that she does so in the name of a higher morality, or, rather, a higher normality, that simply doesn't exist in the film. In fact, by the skewed rules of *Kill Bill*'s universe, Bill's shooting of is almost more just than her revenge. The lazy, dishonestly moralistic about-turn that Tarantino makes with Samuel Jackson's "redemption" in *Pulp Fiction* is ultimately of little consequence amid the self-satisfied posturing of that film because the full extent of its "moral vision" is no more than immanent glibness.

In *Kill Bill*, however, there does exist a playfully challenging system of cinephilic pseudo-values that, for most of the movie, manages to assert itself.

Before lamenting their abandonment, however, we need to ask: in what way are these pseudo-values positive? They are fundamental to the world Tarantino creates in *Kill Bill*. This world exists purely in terms of cinema, completely independently of the real world. While this is, of course, the case with countless genre films, most of them propose an alternative universe, the rules of which we are called on to accept as a substitute reality. In *Kill Bill*, on the other hand, the audience is constantly, winkingly reminded that what it is watching is "only" a movie. This postmodern distance gives rise to if not exactly a critical distance, then a pedagogical one. What *Kill Bill* offers is a lesson in cinema history that unites several genres in a loving, mannerist monument to the films that made Tarantino's cinephilia as powerful a driving force as it evidently is for him. We are not looking at an alternative reality, but an actual existing reality or, rather, realities – those contained in the history of certain movie genres, each with its own folklore and ethical procedures. In his role of self-appointed historian/ambassador to these domains of fiction, Tarantino is – at least up until the aforementioned back-pedalling during the scene of Bill's comeuppance – uninterested in making their customs morally palatable to us citizens of the non-fictional world. The ways of the *chambara* or kung-fu flick or spaghetti Western are not our ways and Tarantino's unique, almost unbalanced degree of respect for these traditions is such that he demands the same from us. The deranged intensity that this attitude generates is the source of *Kill Bill*'s charm – its pseudo-values might be false, but the sincerity of Tarantino's faith in their fantastical power effectively dynamises them.

Let's open a long parenthesis and contextualise *Kill Bill* within Tarantino's oeuvre. *Reservoir Dogs* (1992) was a good movie, lean and intense, a worthy addition to the grand tradition of low-budget American crime cinema. Its director was imaginative and unique enough to have brought that tradition creditably into the '90s. Not a genius like Abel Ferrara or Takashi Miike, but a potentially exciting filmmaker nevertheless. Then he made *Pulp Fiction* (1994) and it all seemed to go wrong. He stopped making generic crime cinema and instead devised the "Tarantino film", an overblown, schizophrenic monster. The good but damagingly overpraised qualities of his debut – a flair for making striking use of known actors both in terms of character and iconic imaging, an interesting grasp of structure, the much celebrated post-modern referentiality of the dialogue that functions to effectively but superficially endow genre characters with a sense of existing in "the real world" – are sufficient to make a genre film interesting but too flimsy for Tarantino to build an entire movie upon, which is what *Pulp Fiction* attempted. The result is crippled with self-consciousness. Every line of dialogue has to be an event. Every plot twist has to be a surprise, but a surprise so carefully worked out that it becomes predictable. With *Pulp Fiction* any sense of spontaneity left Tarantino's cinema never to return.

Tarantino might freely use such expressions as "grindhouse" in describing his work, but he does so from within the safety of the mainstream, never exposing himself to the real dangers and messy pleasures of the B film. His take on genre since *Pulp Fiction* is more like a theme park ride version of "grindhouse" than the real item, a place where actors can flirt with carefully packaged disreputability and come away looking and feeling hip while actually risking nothing. After all, how can a B movie shoulder the responsibility of being a major pop-culture event, which is what is demanded of poor Tarantino every time out? Of course, there is nothing necessarily wrong with creating a hybrid form and, to his credit, Tarantino's films have always remained personal. Yet even with the release of *Jackie Brown* (1997), on many levels an extremely good film, the nagging fantasies persisted of a poorer but more vital Tarantino making a small, ferocious movie every year (assuming that he couldn't make five ferocious movies every year like Miike!) instead of a bloated self-important "event" every four.

He has stated that his films function as generic crime narratives whose traditional progress is interrupted and derailed by the unexpected intervention of events from "real life". However "real life" was never Tarantino's forte. His films deal uniquely with the cinema and, more precisely, his relationship with the cinema. "Real life" is largely signified by the discussion of pop culture which appears to be the only alternative to enacting generic cinema rituals – what is not "cinema" is still defined only in terms of cinema (or music or TV or fast food).

The Tarantino character is not a fully rounded human being as he or she exists neither in relation to others nor to a broader sense of the world, but only to his or her image. Nor is he or she simply a genre type, as those figures are defined by their actions often to the point of being mere pretexts for those actions. Tarantino's creatures are a new and original mutation of the latter: they are defined by the poses they strike of which their actions, like their relationships and even their ethics, are merely functions almost describable as fashion accessories. They are generic archetypes endowed with one human quality: an acute, narcissistic self-consciousness. They don't exist in terms of their acts but of their words and general posturing when interacting. It's all about performance, but a performance that never gets deeper than a posture. When a character speaks, the words do not spring forth from the character so much as the character exists only to utter them. Their self-consciousness is that of an actor playing a role, but there is no sense of a real individual behind the performance.

What is instead present is Tarantino whose voice comes through in every character, every event. Many directors create unique universes that represent their fantasies or visions of the world, but few, if any, are as neurotically, univocally present as Tarantino. In this respect he is closer to stand up comedian than exponent of crime cinema, enacting all the parts in his sketches with one variously modulated voice. Except that Tarantino enacts the parts *through* other actors. He is the phantom actor behind the self-consciously performative tics of his otherwise two-dimensional characters. It is not that he wants to be these characters, but he wants to speak them, act them out – in short, to play at movie gangster. Each character and situation is like a custom-made virtual reality game through which Tarantino can insert himself into cinema. In this way every character becomes a wish fulfillment fantasy for one man, an assortment of iconic figurines personalised through the addition of some everyday quirks. His great good fortune is that, in his physical absence, an audience can pick up on this karaoke ontology and play Tarantino's computer game as well. They can slip into the empty space behind the characters and enjoy their posturing with more than the usual vicarious identification because, unlike in an average Hollywood product, the "game" is so personal. The Tarantino formula doesn't get into your head, you get into its head. You leave yourself behind and move through a carefully designed pattern of behavioural set pieces, often apparently outrageous but never actually dangerous thanks to the taut degree of control exercised over them. The downside of this heavy-duty manipulation, unleavened by the attainment of a visionary state (as in the horror film), is a depressing emotional aridity, a claustrophobia arising from the brutal suppression of the viewer's faculty for forming a free relationship with the world on screen and a relentlessly mechanistic reliance on ultimately grating and empty cleverness. His invitation to a viewer is not the usual one – to look at a/the world through the director's eyes – but to fuse with his mental gestures, gestures that ultimately constrain rather than liberate the audience.

These characteristics were latent in *Reservoir Dogs* but came to dominate in *Pulp Fiction*. Of course *Jackie Brown* transcended these paradigms in many ways – it showed Tarantino capable of genuine gentleness, willing to work with characters that existed beyond the gestural moment with pasts, futures and real relationships. However, at the risk of sounding mean-spirited, perhaps this "mature" Tarantino had simply made a more conventional film? With *Pulp Fiction*, his defining moment as a filmmaker, he had come up with something as unique as it was questionable. With *Jackie Brown*, rather than develop and move forward in terms of the challenges set down by *Pulp Fiction*, he successfully deviated into adaptation which, to play devil's advocate, might seem to represent not a step forward so much as a parenthetical aside in the unfolding Tarantino style. But on another level it represented a very crucial point of transformation between *Pulp Fiction* and *Kill Bill*. It is no longer the "Tarantino monologue" but instead Tarantino engaging with a text, Elmore Leonard's novel. *Jackie Brown* charts the interaction of Tarantino's sensibility with something outside himself, not "real life" but a book that is in itself a pop-culture object. Even if it's only perceptible in post-*Bill* retrospect, the real breakthrough in *Jackie Brown* was the emergence of Tarantino the spectator (or reader) director. It revealed his true talent as a textual filmmaker. He might fail in *Pulp Fiction* at generating a personalised take on "reality" that goes beyond noisily limp post-human caricature, but when he films as a connoisseur and even curator of pop culture "texts" – whether Leonard's book (by way of his concerns with blaxploitation cinema) or his own personal digest of film history in *Bill* – he can be a brilliant and engaging cinematic mind. His undeniable sophistication evidently needs something to engage with outside of itself.

Of course, no two Tarantino films are more different than

Jackie Brown and *Kill Bill*. Through his adaptation of the former, he approached a level of verisimilitude that went beyond that of *Pulp Fiction*. By glammed-up, streamlined Hollywood standards, *Jackie Brown* presents an image of reality that isn't exceptionally stylised. *Bill*, on the other hand, returns to the uniquely "Tarantino world" of *Pulp Fiction* and solves its problems by rejecting any semblance of reality. He has frequently described *Kill Bill* as the film that characters in his previous movies would go and see – a composite fantasy of the "movie-movie". The gangsters, especially in the first two films, are linked to the viewer only by their common consumption of pop culture – both products and consumers, they exist halfway between the audience and the realm of cinema (and television) that haunts these pictures almost like a mythological belief system. *Kill Bill* directly confronts the ontological mystery beyond these characters and explores the mythological underpinnings of their existence. Thus *Kill Bill* is no longer about Tarantino; it is about what Tarantino loves and what he wants to share with us. The annoying posturing and tiring cleverness of *Pulp Fiction* have been replaced by a profound and strangely moving generosity.

Compared to the previous movies, dialogue takes a backseat for much of *Kill Bill*. Its director is now looking rather than talking. Much credit for this development must go to his fetishistic fascination with Uma Thurman. He has, rather touchingly, described the influence of the Sternberg/Dietrich collaboration on his treatment of his star, on the fact that the film is designed entirely to highlight her presence. There has always been an element of playing at filmmaker with Tarantino, as if he were ticking off a list he made when he was about 12 years old of films that he wanted to direct. This time round he is playing at collaborating with "his" actress, at creating an icon. He's found a playmate in his game of cinema, one whose presence has managed to distract him from the sound of his own dialogue. Fortunately, Thurman proves more than worthy of all this attention and embodies the sword-wielding Alice in his Wonderland with exceptional grace and authority. If she is a Jane-of-all-genres, most of the other main characters also function ironically, as the embodiment of a particular genre and the pretext for 's engagement with the tropes and geography of that genre: the *chambara* (Sonny Chiba), the Yakuza movie (Lucy Liu), the kung-fu film (Gordon Liu), the Western (Michael Madsen), the blaxploitation picture (Vivica A. Fox). In Bill, or, rather, in David Carradine, star of both *The Long Riders* (Walter

Hill, 1980) and the *Kung Fu* TV series, the traditions of the Western and Martial Arts cinemas are neatly united. He incarnates the cultural fusion that the whole movie attempts.

The difference between these overtly monumental characters and those in previous Tarantino films becomes most obvious in that unfortunate Bride/Bill confrontation scene which we will return to simply in order to highlight its difference from the rest of the picture – and its incongruous similarity to the previous work. As soon as their daughter is safely asleep, the antagonists start talking. They talk at great length, in so doing basically going over everything that we have been shown over the course of the film, over-emphasising, over-explaining. It is the only occasion when dialogue is not tied to unfolding events, to movement, to action. The Bill-Bride relationship was already admirably summarised in a wonderful scene in church during her wedding rehearsal, just before he shoots her. Not only is the dialogue here redundant on an expositional level but it reveals a serious underestimation of the actors on Tarantino's part. Their expressivity is such that a few looks and gestures would have been more than sufficient to convey everything that needs saying with much greater feeling than all the scene's verbose hot air. Worst of all, their verbal expressions are often woefully inappropriate. It's as if the prospect of finding an adequate conclusion to *Kill Bill* scared Tarantino to such an extent that his only recourse was to drag every Tarantino party trick out of the closet. Or maybe he believed that the audience would feel cheated if they didn't have enough of the requisite "Tarantino dialogue". Either way, the result is close to self-parody. Tarantino's voice starts speaking through Bill and ; they talk like characters from *Pulp Fiction*. But whereas the earlier film was entirely built on Tarantino's univocality, the effect here is that the words overwhelm the characters and their predicament. Even the actors' delivery seems suddenly excessively smug, heavy with the knowledge that every word spoken adds another gem of Tarantino's smartness to the grateful setting of popular culture. The problem is that this manner of speech, as described above, sets the character midway between the audience and the world of "movie-movie", which *Kill Bill* emphatically inhabits. It is blindingly obvious that Bill and were born to be "superheroes", to be different from ordinary people. There's no need for Bill to verbalize that and certainly not as an embarrassing, pseudo-philosophical dissertation on Superman comics. Such a speech would not be out of place in the mouths of

John Travolta or Samuel Jackson in *Pulp Fiction*, existing as do they between viewer and generic archetype. But hearing it from David Carradine, with all Bill's gravitas, is almost grotesque, as if Superman himself suddenly started imitating Tarantino!

Fortunately, elsewhere in the film the dialogue, while recognizably Tarantino's, remains appropriately the language of "superheroes" and elegantly functional. The conclusion notwithstanding, *Kill Bill* is the first of his films plotted in such a way that he doesn't need to rely on smart dialogue, with expertly executed action based set-pieces taking centre stage. With every major character representing a genre, 's almost invariably violent encounter with each antagonist is Tarantino's way of invoking and even explaining those genres and thus creating a stylistic plurality that renders the univocality of his previous films undesirable. The indexical nature of the characters is crucial to *Kill Bill*'s daffy grandeur. They don't simply happen to be from different cultures and fighting traditions. If that were the case, there would be little difference between 's journey and the sleazy, neo-imperialist action movie tourism of James Bond. Tarantino's assortment of killers is more than characters, more than products of different film styles: they are conscious symbols of their genre and carry with them the weight of its history. Their interaction amounts to nothing less than clashes between the entirety of the cinematic traditions that they represent. Thus, these battles are able to assume an importance that feels grander than the immediate narrative predicament. An example of this dynamic: in part two goes to kill westerner Budd (Michael Madsen). She goes with her sword at night and hides under his mobile home, ninja style. Upon breaking into the trailer, she finds him waiting for her, shotgun at the ready. He wounds and captures her without a struggle. One up for the Western! Then, in the macabre tradition of the Italian Western, we learn that her fate is to be buried alive in a graveyard (although effective, this interment scene is notable as the only mannerist set-piece in the film that the essentially prosaic imagist Tarantino doesn't get the maximum out of visually – one could imagine an Italian director milking it for much more gothic visual poetry). Once six feet under, the heroine overcomes her despair by mentally flashing back to her period of training with martial arts master Pai Mei (Gordon Liu) that took place in the grainy, zoom-rich, bleached out colour of a '70s kung-fu flick. Drawing on the techniques she picked up in China, she is able to literally punch her way out of the grave. Thus the martial arts movie beats the Western in this round. Her emergence from the ground is given a comic punchline that links it to the zombie subgenre – looking every bit like she just crawled out of a grave, she wanders into a late night diner and asks the startled waiter for a glass of water! If *Kill Bill* has a truly epic dimension, it is born of this clash of traditions, the battle of film histories. The density of *Kill Bill*'s cinematic esoterica also differentiates it from the "image karaoke" of the *Charlie's Angels* or *Austin Powers* movies – almost post-genre comedies where the history of cinema has become no more than a trunk of fancy dress outfits in the attic to be raided at whim.

Death and rebirth are at the heart of *Kill Bill*'s vision of cinema: the vulnerability and resilience of genres that are all essentially dead. They exist either completely in the past or else the era of their history that *Kill Bill* specifically cites is no more. Cycles of revenge dominate the structure of the film: Bill's shooting of The Bride, Vernita's daughter's possible future revenge against The Bride for her mother's death's, the massacre of O-Ren Ishii's parents that turned her into a killer. The nature of revenge: one moment of the past played and replayed obsessively to the point of excluding present reality – the absolute domination of a past that not only won't go away but is not allowed to go away. Perhaps *Kill Bill* is the past of certain cinemas come back to take revenge on the collective mainstream of cinematic memory that has almost forgotten them. Rebirth against all odds is also central to *Kill Bill*. However much punishment she takes, keeps coming back – shot in the head, raped, buried alive, drugged, battered several times over, she refuses to let herself die. Her persistence is at once the persistence of basic cinematic narratives that won't go away, like the revenge story, and their destruction: her quest is, after all, to systematically eradicate film genres that are already, in fact, dead and, ultimately, to save her daughter from the clutches of cinema, to return her to a normal reality where the formal relics through which she has fought can find no nourishment. Yet is her murder of a little girl's mother at the film's opening not perhaps a booby trap that could one day result in her own death and the recommencement of the endless cycle of revenge with her now apparently safe daughter? Is the normality of their family life going to be any less of a Buñuelesque sham than Vernita's was? Might not one day a flow of blood again lead to a flow of images, memory images of a cinema past that, vampire-like, is waiting to leap anew into spectral action at the first drop? The image of the violent murder of loved ones, the indelible image of violence that leaves an after-image so potent that it must be pursued forever after, here doubles as the cinematic experience, as the cinephile Tarantino witnessing his own unforgettable images of violence in the cinema and pursuing them until he had replicated them. William Witney, Kinji Fukasaku, Charles Bronson and the other names on the list of the dead in the closing credits might be no more, but the narrative echoes of the films they participated in carry on endlessly, perpetuating themselves in a void that now exists beyond time and which can be accessed only through memory – or the refusal to forget. This is the space that *Kill Bill* articulates.

The fragility of life, or, rather, of the images which sustain the lives in *Kill Bill* is constantly highlighted: Vernita's wrecked household, the snow-covered garden appearing behind the Tokyo nightclub, 's new family-to-(never)-be wiped out in the church, the apparently washed up Budd's unexpected ambush, the snake that bites him hidden in the case of money, Bill's assumed superiority in martial arts undermined by … This fragility does not merely reflect the constant threat of death or the deceptive nature of appearances, but the thinness of those appearances and the emptiness behind them, their lack of roots in reality. Like the characters in *Pulp Fiction*, those in *Kill Bill* exist only through their image, but this time around Tarantino acknowledges the fact and its consequences and, crucially, links their faux-existentialist predicament to the memory of cinema past. In the act of acknowledging the disappearance of these cinemas, Tarantino causes them to live again and die again. But this death is never final because even if a character is truly done for, it only takes another killing and the endlessly renewable forces of basic narrative will start the whole pageant again with an equivalent character built of the same image, an image as indestructible as the host-character is disposable… It could be in the studios of Hollywood or Shanghai, on the streets of Tokyo or Hong Kong, in the deserts of Almeria… It could be the '70s, it could be now, the '60s, the future… It could be a memorable film or we might forget it immediately. But at least we can do so in the knowledge that Quentin Tarantino, an interesting filmmaker and a priceless film historian, is probably remembering it for us.

BIBLIOGRAPHY

Andrew, Geoff: *Stranger Than Paradise: Maverick Film-Makers In Recent American Cinema*, Limelight Editions, New York, 1999.

Barnes, Alan, and Marcus Hearn: *Tarantino A To Zed: The Films of Quentin Tarantino*, B. T. Batsford Ltd., London, 1999.

Bernard, Jami: *Quentin Tarantino: The Man And His Movies*, HarperPerrenial, New York, 1995.

Billson, Anne: *The Thing*, B.F.I. Publishing, London, 1997.

Bordwell, David: *Planet Hong Kong: Popular Cinema And The Art Of Entertainment*, Harvard University Press, Cambridge, 2000.

Biskind, Peter: *Down And Dirty Pictures: Miramax, Sundance, and The Rise Of Independent Film*, Simon and Schuster, New York, 2004.

Bukatman, Scott: *Blade Runner*, B.F.I. Publishing, London, 1997.

Burns, Tom: *Erving Goffman*, Routledge, London, 1992.

Buscombe, Edward: *The Searchers*, B.F.I. Publishing, London, 2000.

Byron, Stuart: *"The Searchers*: Cult Movie of the New Hollywood," *New York,* March 5, 1979, pages 45-48.

Callow, Simon: *The Night of the Hunter*, B.F.I. Publishing, London, 2000.

Clarkson Wensley: *Quentin Tarantino: Shooting From The Hip*, Overlook, Woodstock, 1995.

Clements, Jonathan, and Helen McCarthy: *The Anime Encyclopedia: A Guide To Japanese Animation Since 1917*, Stone Bridge Press, Berkeley, 2001.

Clements, Jonathan, and Motoko Tamamuro: *The Dorama Encyclopedia: A Guide To Japanese TV Drama Since 1953*, Stone Bridge Press, Berkeley, 2004.

Coker, Cheo Hodari: "View To A Kill," *Premiere,* September 2003, page 64.

Cooke, Bill: "*Kill Bill Vol. 1*," *Video Watchdog,* August 2004, pages 40 – 45.

Dannen, Fredric, and Barry Long: *Hong Kong Babylon: An Insider's Guide to the Hollywood of the East*, Miramax, New York, 1997.

Dawson, Jeff: *Quentin Tarantino: The Cinema Of Cool*, Applause, New York, 1995.

Durgnat, Raymond, and Scott Simmon: *King Vidor, American*, University of California Press, Berkeley, 1988.

Durgnat, Raymond: *A Long Hard Look At Psycho*, B.F.I. Publishing, London, 200x.

Durgnat, Raymond: *Sexual Alienation In The Cinema*, Studio Vista, London, 1972.

Feiffer, Jules: *The Great Comic Book Heroes*, Dial, New York, 1965.

Fierman, Daniel: "The Kill Zone," *Entertainment Weekly*, October 3, 2003, pages 24-35.

Fonoroff, Paul: *At The Hong Kong Movies*, Film Biweekly, Hong Kong, 1998.

Frayling, Christopher: *Spaghetti Westerns: Cowboys and Europeans From Karl May to Sergio Leone*, Tauris, London, 1998.

Fu, Poshek, and David Desser: *The Cinema Of Hong Kong: History, Arts, Identity*, Cambridge University Press, Cambridge, 2000.

Goffman, Erving: *The Presentation Of Self In Everyday Life*, Anchor Press, Garden City, 1959.

Graham, Gini Scott: *Dominant Women Submissive Men: An Exploration In Erotic Dominance and Submission*, Praeger, New York, 1983.

Gross, Michael: *Model: The Ugly Business Of Beautiful Women*, Morrow, New York, 1994.

Hall, Kenneth E.: *John Woo: The Films*, McFarland, Jefferson, 1999.

Hammond, Stefan, and Mike Wilkins: *Sex, Zen and a Bullet in the Head: The Essential Guide To Hong Kong's Mind-Bending Films*, Fireside, New York, 1996.

Hamsher, Jane: *Killer Instinct: How Two Young Producers Took On Hollywood And Made The Most Controversial Film Of The Decade*, Broadway Books, New York, 1997.

Hanke, Ken: *Charlie Chan at the Movies: History, Filmography, and Criticism*, McFarland, 1989.

Hardy, Phil: *The Western: The Aurum Film Encyclopedia*, Aurum, London, 1991.

Hedegaard, Erik: "A Magnificent Obsession," *Rolling Stone*, 29 April 2004, pages 40 – 50.

Hidalgo, Pablo: "The Wilhelm Scream," <http://cgi.theforce.net/theforce/tfn.cgi? storyID=5312>

Holm, D.K.: *Quentin Tarantino*, Pocket Essentials, Harpenden, 2004.

Hughes, Howard: *Spaghetti Westerns*, Pocket Essentials, Harpenden, 2001.

Kapp, Leon and Hiroko and Yoshindo Yoshihara: *The Craft Of The Japanese Sword,* Kodansha, New York, 1987.

Katz, Ephraim: *The Film Encyclopedia: Third Edition*, HarperCollins, New York, 1997.

Knowles, Harry: "Harry talks to Quentin Tarantino about KILL BILL, GLORIOUS BASTARDS and QTV!!!," Ain't It Cool News.com <http://www.aintitcool.com/display.cgi? id=9830 >, August 10, 2001.

Lemert, Charles, and Ann Branaman: *The Goffman Reader*, Blackwell, London, 1997.

Levy, Emanuel: *Cinema Of Outsiders: The Rise Of American Independent Film*, New York University Press, New York and London, 1999.

Lyman, Rick: *Watching Movies: The Biggest Names In Cinema Talk About The Films That Matter Most*, Times Books, New York, 2002.

Lyons, Donald: "Scumbags," *Film Comment*, November–December 1992, pages 6, 8.

MacFarquhar, Larissa: "The Movie Lover," *The New Yorker*, October 20 2003, page 146.

Malloy, Mike: Lee Van Clef: A Biographical, Film, and Television Reference, McFarland, Jefferson, 1998.

Martin. Michael: "Princess Bride," *Arena*, November 2003, pages 118 – 127.

MarvelDirectory.com: "Serpent Society," <http://www.marveldirectory.com/teams/ serpentsociety.htm>.

Massey, James, and Shirley Maxwell: *House Styles in America: The Old-House Journal Guide to the Architecture of American Homes*, Penguin, New York, 1996.

McCarty, John and Brian Kelleher: *Alfred Hitchcock Presents: An Illustrated Guide To The Ten-Year Television Career Of The Master Of Suspense*, St. Martin's Press, New York, 1984.

McCarthy, Todd: "*Kill Bill Vol. 1*," *Variety*, posted September 30, 2003, <http://www.variety.com/ac2004_review/VE1117921975?nav=reviews&categoryid=1657&cs=1&query=kill+and+bill+and+vol%2E+and+1&display=kill+bill+vol%2E+1>.

Mes, Tom: *Agitator: The Cinema of Takashi Miike*, Fab Press, Godalming, 2003.

Mally, Mike: *Lee Van Cleef: A Biographical, Film and Television Reference*, McFarland, Jefferson, 1998.

Mustafa, Tony: "*Shogun Assassin*" < http://dvdcult.com/rev_ShogunA.htm>

Newman, Kim: "*Kill Bill Vol. 1*," *Sight and Sound*, August 1994.

Olsen, Mark: "Turning On A Dime," *Sight And Sound*, December 2003, pages 39 – 42.

Pavlus, John: "A Bride Vows Revenge," *American Cinematographer*, October 2003, pages 34 – 47.

Peary, Gerald: *Quentin Tarantino: Interviews*, University Press of Mississippi, Jackson, 1998.

Polan, Dana: *Pulp Fiction: BFI Modern Classics*, BFI Publishing, London, 2000.

Pollard, Mark: "*Shogun's Samurai*," <http://www.kungfucinema.com/reviews/ shogunssamurai.htm >.

Rich, B. Ruby: "Day Of The Woman," *Sight And Sound*, June 2004, pages 24 – 27.

Robertson, Patrick: *Film Facts*, Billboard Books, New York, 2001.

Sarris, Andrew: *The American Cinema: Directors and Directions, 1929 – 1968*, William Witney, Dutton, New York, 1968.

Sato, Kanzan: *The Japanese Sword*, Kodansha, New York, 1983.

Schilling, Mary Kaye: "The Second Coming," *Entertainment Weekly*, August 16 2004, pages 24 – 30.

Schilling, Mark: *The Yakuza Movie Book*, Stone Bridge Press, Berkeley, 2003.

Schruers, Fred: "The Moviegoer," *Premiere*, May 2004, pages 74 -78, 119.

Sharff, Stefan: *The Art Of Looking In Hitchcock's* Rear Window, Limelight Editions, New York, 1997.

Silver, Alain: *The Samurai Book*, Overlook, Woodstock, 1983.

Silver, Alain: "Violence, East and West: *The Last Samurai*," Senses of Cinema.com,
<http://www.sensesofcinema.com/contents/04/30/last_samurai.html>.

Smith, Jim: *Gangster Films*, Virgin, London, 2004.

Stokes, Lisa Odham, and Michael Hoover: *City On Fire: Hong Kong Cinema*, Verso, London, 1999.

Teo, Stephen: *Hong Kong Cinema: The Extra Dimension*, B.F.I. Publishing, London, 1997.

Thomas, Brian: *VideoHound's Dragon: Asian Action and Cult Flicks*, Visible Ink, Detroit, 2003.

Theroux, Alexander: *Darconville's Cat*, Doubleday, Garden City, 1981.

Theroux, Alexander: "Revenge," *Harpers*, October, 198, pages 26 – 31.

"Topher's Breakfast Cereal Character Guide"
<http://www.lavasurfer.com/cereal-generalmills5.html>

Weaver, Ken: *Texas Crude*, Dutton, New York, 1984.

Weisser, Thomas: *Spaghetti Westerns: The Good, The Bad and the Violent: 558 Eurowesterns and their Personnel, 1961 – 1977*, McFarland, Jefferson, 2003.

Weisser, Thomas, and Yuko Mihara Weisser: *Japanese Cinema Essential Handbook, 5th Edition*, Vital, Miami, 2003.

Williams, David E.: "Gone To The Dogs," *Film Threat,* Issue No. 17, August 1994.

Winter, Douglas E.: *Run*, Knopf, New York, 2000.

Wise, Damon: *"Kill Bill Uncut,"* Empire Online
<http://www.empireonline.co.uk/site/
features/special/killbill/default.asp#kil>

Witney, William: *In A Door, Into A Fight, Out A Door, Into A Chase*, McFarland, Jefferson, 1996.

Wood, Miles: *Cine East: Hong Kong Cinemas Through the Looking Glass*, Fab Press, Surrey, 1998.

Wood, Robin: *Howard Hawks*, B.F.I. Publishing, London, 1981.

Wood, Robin: *Rio Bravo*, B.F.I. Publishing, London, 2003.

Woods, Paul A.: *King Pulp: The Wild World of Quentin Tarantino*, Thunder's Mouth Press, New York, 1996.

Woods, Paul A.: *Quentin Tarantino: The Film Geek Files*, Plexus, London, 2000.

Wright, Evan: "Quentin's Kung Fu Grip," *Rolling Stone*, October 30 2003, pages 42-46.

Yau, Esther C. M., Editor: *At Full Speed: Hong Kong Cinema In A Borderless World*, University of Minnesota Press, Minnesota, 2001.

Zalcock, Bev: *Renegade Sisters: Girl Gangs On Film*, Creation Books, London and San Francisco, revised edition, 2000.